Interculturality and the Munchausen Effect

This book offers a conceptual intervention for Language and Intercultural Communication studies by advocating for a critical interdiscursive approach to research on interculturality.

The volume addresses two interrelated theses in research on interculturality; namely that the speaking subject in interaction reproduces the egocentrism and phonocentrism of the Munchausen Effect. In considering the first, the book traces the ways in which interculturality research has historically supposed the 'speaking subject'—that is, the research participant—as the basis of truth and knowledge, not giving context to the discursive layers or paratexts involved in analyzing the subject's speech. This notion of the 'speaking subject' being taken at face value prompts Simpson's second interrelated argument on representation and historical conceptualizations of community in interculturality research, whereby, in trying to represent their subjects, researchers often impose a sense of community affiliation onto their subjects and end up negating their subjective identities. The book serves as a conceptual and practical response to calls for epistemological diversity and plurality within Interculturality in proposing an approach that brings epistemology and ontology together.

This book will be of interest to scholars in intercultural communication, language education, identity theory, and philosophy of education.

Ashley Simpson is Lecturer in Language Education at Moray House School of Education and Sport, University of Edinburgh, UK. Ashley Simpson is also Co-Head of the Institute of Language Education at Moray House School of Education and Sport, University of Edinburgh, UK.

Routledge Studies in Language and Intercultural Communication

Edited by Zhu Hua, *Birkbeck College, University of London*
Claire Kramsch, *University of California, Berkeley*

Decolonizing Applied Linguistics Research i Latin America
Moving to a Multilingual Mindset
Edited by Harold Castañeda-Peña, Paola Gamboa and Claire Kramsch

Communicative Perspectives on COVID-19 in Ghana
At the Intersection of Culture, Science, Religion and Politics
Edited by Nancy Henaku, G. Edzordzi Agbozo and Mark Nartey

Expanding Ecological Approaches to Language, Culture, and Identity
Politics and Power in South Korean Multicultural Youths' Experiences
Jaran Shin

Material Interculturality
Making Sense with Everyday Objects
Cristina Ros i Solé

Interculturality and the Munchausen Effect
On the Need to Rethink the Speaking Subject and Community in Interaction
Ashley Simpson

https://www.routledge.com/Routledge-Studies-in-Language-and-Intercultural-Communication/book-series/LICC

Interculturality and the Munchausen Effect

On the Need to Rethink the Speaking Subject and Community in Interaction

Ashley Simpson

NEW YORK AND LONDON

First published 2025
by Routledge
605 Third Avenue, New York, NY 10158

and by Routledge
4 Park Square, Milton Park, Abingdon, Oxon, OX14 4RN

Routledge is an imprint of the Taylor & Francis Group, an informa business

© 2025 Ashley Simpson

The right of Ashley Simpson to be identified as author of this work has been asserted in accordance with sections 77 and 78 of the Copyright, Designs and Patents Act 1988.

All rights reserved. No part of this book may be reprinted or reproduced or utilised in any form or by any electronic, mechanical, or other means, now known or hereafter invented, including photocopying and recording, or in any information storage or retrieval system, without permission in writing from the publishers.

Trademark notice: Product or corporate names may be trademarks or registered trademarks, and are used only for identification and explanation without intent to infringe.

ISBN: 9781032255224 (hbk)
ISBN: 9781032255248 (pbk)
ISBN: 9781003283713 (ebk)

DOI: 10.4324/9781003283713

Typeset in Times New Roman
by Newgen Publishing UK

For Cyprian, Tikhon and Ustinia.

Contents

1 Introduction 1

2 Interculturality and the Problem of the Speaking Subject 21

3 Interculturality, Representation and the Munchausen Effect 33

4 Interculturality and Commodification: The Fetishisation of Social Relations 47

5 Interculturality and the Commons 79

6 Conclusion: Reconfiguring Interculturality Within the Dialectics of the Everyday 105

Bibliography *114*
Index *127*

1 Introduction

Theoretical positioning of this book

The notion of the 'Intercultural' arguably dates back to the 1950s (e.g. the work of Edward T. Hall [1959]) – although many of the ideas that the Intercultural encompasses have, of course, a much longer history. In over 70 years and in the different fields that have used the notion, as one would expect, the 'Intercultural' has witnessed changes in the way it is defined, constructed, researched, practiced. However, the Intercultural has also retained some of its original flavours (e.g. culturalism, see Abdallah-Pretceille, 2006). As a highly ideological notion, the 'Intercultural' has been used in different ways across the globe and is sometimes interchangeably used with other notions and concepts such as multicultural, transcultural and even global. Today, it is commonplace to find 'mainstream' research on the Intercultural associating the notion with 'assessing' and/or acquiring particular socio-linguistic competences and skills (e.g. Byram, 2021; Deardorff, 2019). These versions of the Intercultural can be translated socially and politically in terms of reflecting a modernist version of 'the Intercultural' that is based upon what people *are* or what they *ought* to be and can reflect the reproduction of mainstream ('liberal') socio-political ideologies through normative values, concepts and knowledge (R'boul, 2021).

Though in more recent times, voices from peripheral perspectives and contexts in terms of the conceptual positioning of research on the Intercultural are seemingly being heard little by little (Guilherme & de Souza, 2019; Simpson & Dervin, 2020). Supranational institutions like the European Union and the Council of Europe (2018), continue

DOI: 10.4324/9781003283713-1

to produce and reproduce a particular form of the Intercultural, passing onto researchers and practitioners a certain number of biases, stereotypes and uncritically reflexive positions, failing to recognise the geopolitical space that they cover (Dervin & Simpson, 2021).

It is thus important to pay attention to the historical developments of the Intercultural that can be understood, e.g. through the shift from 'the comparative and culture-as-nation research agenda to a discourse perspective to intercultural communication' (Zhu, 2020: 207). Inspired by the discourse perspective of Intercultural Communication (Kramsch & Zhu, 2016) this book conceptualises Intercultural interactions through the notion of Interculturality – Interculturality is understood as 'the dynamic actioning between the self and others. The notion corresponds to the plain across, and within, which dialogues between the self and other are performed, negotiated and co-constructed' (Dervin & Simpson, 2021: 23). Thus, Interculturality is neither a fixed state nor is it a marker of a singular event or situation (i.e. an objectivised spatial or temporal totality) nor is it a marker for self-identification (i.e. *x* is 'my culture', 'I come from country *y*' or 'I am a speaker of *z*') (Dervin & Simpson, 2021). Yet, there are constraints upon the self-other relationship meaning there is always a perpetual sense of outsideness – meaning no stable evaluative position can ever be maintained between self and other (Simpson, 2022). In research on Interculturality, this tension can be reflected by a mismatch between analytical tools and philosophical approaches, or in ways research participants are often generalised contrary to the theoretical approach of the researcher (see, Holliday & MacDonald's [2020] discussion on how postpositivist research approaches to Intercultural Communication can reproduce othering and neoracism).

Zhu Hua correctly identifies in *Research Methods in Intercultural Communication: A Practical Guide* (2016) research on Intercultural Communication encompasses a broad range of disciplines, approaches and methods which often criss-cross one another. Giuliana Ferri (2018: 4–5) goes further in showing that there is no unified methodological approach to Interculturality due to the array of complexities being studied. Yet, Interculturality is inherently positivist in the ways some methods, approaches and theories are applied (Ferri, 2018). As a result, research on Interculturality can sometimes be characterised by empirical and methodological deficiencies such as: Eurocentric biases – the discourse of skills and competencies for the conflict management of self and other; Essentialism – the other is marked according to closed boundaries and categories such as culture, nationality or language; Assumptions of difference – similar to what Dervin (2016) calls a differentialist bias, whereby difference becomes an analytical marker rather than an analysis based on similarities and differences; and, a focus on micro-level practices – research is based on communicative practices in small group situations (Ferri, 2018).

Research on Interculturality which falls within these domains can also contribute to the production and reproduction of methodological nationalism – whereby researchers focus on representatives of one country/context rather than looking at experiences of people from other contexts (Dervin & Simpson, 2021). In this sense, researchers can bind their research participants to specific political, social, linguistic or geographic boundaries which they cannot escape, i.e. the research subjects become 'boxed in'. In this sense, boundaries (translated in research as categories or labels) become (assumed) markers for what the research participant belongs to or identifies towards. For example, a research subject may be labelled as a 'migrant' by the researcher in a study and they might find it difficult to remove the discursive shackles of the concept. Conversely, a research participant in a study may self-identify themselves as being British and this label can negate a multifaceted and fluid perspective through which their identity may be constructed. In both examples, the multiple identities of the self are reduced down to a label, a category, an essence. These concepts and labels have no agency in themselves but deployed in essentialising ways they can strip the agency from the subject in research on Interculturality. In a journal article, Kjetil Fretheim (2021) demonstrates there is a growing need to critically analyse established labels and go under the discursive surface of Interculturality research to move beyond the production and reproduction of superficial simplicity.

There is also a need to challenge epistemological research developments such as positivism and postpositivism which simplify complexity and engender dichotomic discourses in research on Interculturality (Fretheim, 2021). Along similar lines, Holliday & MacDonald (2020) argue that postpositivist methodologies, characterised by the popularity of interpretivist approaches to research on Interculturality have contributed to the othering of research subjects. Othering means turning a subject into an object through essentialist discourses and/or representations. For Holliday and MacDonald one of the problems lies, for example, in deploying qualitative research tools such as interviews the utterances of the interviewee are taken as a form of 'objective knowledge' by the researcher. Thus, the interviewer/researcher takes the interviewee's word 'as a given' insofar that their utterances demonstrate some form of knowledge and/or truth about Interculturality. Researchers' othering their research participants can be problematic when interpreting and translating research data from multiple languages and dealing with differing degrees of translatable and untranslatable material (Ruitenberg et al., 2016). In recent years, the role of the researcher in Interculturality has been placed under the microscope in terms of acknowledging and questioning the power relations, ideologies and influence that researchers exert over the research process; analysing the role of the researcher means critically analysing the researchers' roles, utterances and behaviour in a dialogic and reflexive manner (Dervin & Simpson, 2021). Understanding the research process from an interactive and dialogic perspective, for example, through analysing how the interviewee and interviewer co-construct and negotiate meaning in interaction, does not necessarily prevent othering or essentialist representations from being produced or reproduced – as these discourses can still be superimposed onto the self and/or other. Methodological symptoms of the critical and reflexive turn (Dasli & Diaz, 2017) in Interculturality are illustrated here, insofar that criticality and reflexivity have conceptual limitations (when conceptualised exclusively from the position of self rather than the position of self-other), and that there is somewhat of an overspill of 'critical' research on Interculturality which means the many notions contained in research on Interculturality are inherently polysemic and have many uses. By 'overspill' here I refer to the number of critical perspectives and approaches used in Interculturality research (I am certainly not suggesting there should be one unified critical approach, rather, that critical perspectives are seemingly 'popular' at this given time), yet such approaches can lead to the epistemological privilege of knowledge over ontology (see., Bhaskar, 2008) of certain discourses in terms of what critical research on Interculturality entails and what the wider social purpose of such research should be for (Dasli & Diaz, 2017). The dangers of *acritical* and anachronic Interculturality have been documented whereby such research can serve to reinforce dominant hegemonies, ideologies or ways of thinking about Interculturality instead of addressing and redressing the ways epistemologies and ontologies about Interculturality are mediated through wider societal processes and systems (Simpson & Dasli, 2023). But, perhaps, one needs to stop, pause, and think – what if this epoch of 'Critical Interculturality' has not yet emerged, or perhaps, it cannot emerge. Perhaps it would be naïve to categorically argue that Interculturality has turned fully to a point of criticality (Simpson & Dasli, 2023).

Why I decided to write this book

The inspiration for this book was derived from a number of academic journal articles I had been asked to review for different academic journals over the past few years. In my reviewer comments, time and time again I was asking the author[s] to clarify and critically reflect upon how they were presenting the research subjects in the paper. This comment was not exclusive to qualitative studies using interview or focus group research tools whereby researchers were 'stating' what their research participants were 'telling them' (rather than critically analysing their utterances) but was also relevant to quantitative methodological papers which used statistics to generalise individuals and/or groups in research on Interculturality. In both qualitative and quantitative approaches (I am not presenting qualitative and quantitative research in such a binary manner as the boundaries between these approaches are often blurry and researchers can use both approaches in mixed methods research) the author[s] were seemingly taking what their research participants were saying 'at face value' without delving beyond the surface appearance of the given discourses and/or representations. Seemingly, the word of *the speaking subject* was time and time again taken as a given. The concept of the *speaking subject* refers to the semantic processes through which language systems are embodied through enunciative acts, i.e. utterances made by individuals (Pêcheux, 1982).

In this sense, as a reviewer, how could I know if the research participant *actually* said these things? Or if they did say them, in what discursive context did they say them and how did they say them? For example, it was unclear what utterances preceded the reported utterances beforehand and what followed on afterwards by both interviewee and interviewer – instead I was offered a snapshot of what the interviewee supposedly said. There was no analysis of differing discursive layers or paratexts which were integrated into the analysis of the reported speech. This was the first part of the 'problem' which kept on recurring time and time again.

The speaking subject being taken at face value raised another 'problem': the problem of representation. In the instances where the researcher was taking their interviewees' utterances at face value, who was representing the subject? The authors were stating in their research that they were representing their research participants (often critically and reflexively) yet the labels and categorises they used about their research participants seemingly 'boxed' them in and meant that it was conceptually difficult for their research participants to be represented beyond the labels and categories the researcher gave the research participant. Whether the research participant was a migrant or refugee, whether they were British or Chinese, whether it was the author[s] voice or the voice of the research participants (which they often claimed), it seemed the speaking subject in the research was being turned into an object. It was commonplace to find the speaking subject's discourses were used to essentialise itself through assuming the speaking subject identified or belonged to a specific community (whether that be a 'national community' based on nationality, a 'linguistic community' based on the languages the speaker spoke, or 'cultural community' based on what 'culture' the speaker belonged to). In this sense, community demarked how the speaking subject was represented and what they belonged to, which was seemingly not problematised in depth in the research. Or, if community happened to be discussed in the research papers it turned the speaking subject into an object of research on Interculturality by equating the speakers' utterances to specific concepts (e.g. as an 'Intercultural speaker' or through the dichotomies of native speakerism and non-native speakerism) which encloses the subjective identities of the subjects being represented in the studies.

With these considerations in mind, this book addresses the following two interrelated arguments. The first, research on Interculturality, has been predominantly conceptualised through the 'speaking subject' which incorrectly posits the subject as the basis and origin of all knowledge. This conceptualisation of the speaking subject assumes that the subject is free and rational 'to speak the truth'. The second interrelated argument which this book argues is: The historical conceptualisation of community in research on Interculturality negates the identity of the subject. In this sense, due to the primacy of the speaking subject, research on Interculturality imposes a sense of community onto the subject from outside of the self through 'objective' representations which negate a plural and fluid approach to identity.

Thus, this book aims to problematise the role of the speaking subject and the role of community in conceptualising a dialectical perspective for research on Interculturality.

The speaking subject and the Munchausen Effect

To fully problematise the speaking subject in research on Interculturality one must first problematise how subjectification manifests through discourse and in interaction. In their work on Intercultural Communication Scollon et al., (2012) succinctly discuss the ways discourse systems about gender and sexuality can reify (i.e. objectify and essentialise) the identities of individuals. In this sense, discourse systems (and discursive acts) are not 'natural' – discourses are mediated by social forces and systems that need to be contextualised within historical processes. In *Language, Semantics and Ideology: Stating the Obvious* (1982) the French philosopher and linguist Michel Pêcheux articulates this problematique through the 'Munchausen Effect' (Pêcheux, 1982: 108), meaning 'ideology recruits subjects from amongst individuals and that it recruits them all' (ibid.). For Pêcheux, the Munchausen Effect is understood through the following quotation:

> In what concerns us, how all individuals accept as evident the meaning of what they hear and say, read and write (of what they intend to say and of what it is intended be said to them) as 'speaking subjects': really to understand this is the only way to avoid repeating, in the form of a theoretical analysis, the 'Munchausen effect', by positing the subject as the origin of the subject. (Pêcheux, 1982: 109)

In engaging in French Philosopher Louis Althusser's work on *Ideology and Ideological State Apparatuses* (2014) (which was first published in 1970), Pêcheux (1982) articulates the problem is the subject-form: an assumption that the practice of the subject belongs to the subject (i.e. the subject's actions, activities, behaviour) and that s/he is the responsible author of those acts and is thus interpellated as a responsible subject. Pêcheux argues that discourse, in this view, is never at one with itself (Angermuller et al., 2014). Thus, language cannot be conceptualised as a window to the external world or to an internal consciousness. Instead, language is perceived as a surface of opaque signs whose constraints on interpretive activities need to be decrypted (Angermuller, 2018).

Individuals are thus interpellated as speaking subjects through ideology (Pêcheux, 1982), or as Althusser (2014) puts it, the existence of ideology and the interpellation of the individuals as subjects are one and the same thing. This identification is always preconstructed '(the "always-already" there of the ideological interpellation that supplies-imposes "reality" and its "meaning" in the form of universality the "world of things")' (Pêcheux, 1982: 156). For Pêcheux subjectification and the subjugation of the subject as an ideological subject are connected so that everyone is led, without realising it, and with a limited sense of exercising her/his free will (Angermuller et al., 2014).

The subject can never therefore proclaim, in echoing Rene Descartes, I think therefore I am (*Cogito ergo sum*) (Descartes, 1968), for Pêcheux this argument is rendered impotent as 'subjects do not say what they mean, their discourse is unconsciously dominated by interdiscourse, through which they are constituted' (Maingueneau, 2011: 110). Interdiscourse (which is closely akin to the philosopher and literary critic Mikhail Bakhtin's [2012] work on polyphony and dialogism) as a principle rejects any approach that would consider discursive identities to be closed domains. Discourses are conceptualised through a constant process of being determined – thus, discourses are always criss-crossed by manifold forms of other discourses (Maingueneau, 2011).

Pêcheux's approach to language and discourse seemingly resonates with Valentin Voloshinov's (1973) work on *Marxism and the Philosophy of Language* and Mikhail Bakhtin's (1981; 2012) work on authoritative discourse and externally persuasive discourse. Authoritative discourse can relate to discursive traditions, customs, and ignorance (Matusov, 2007) whereas internally persuasive discourse is akin to retelling a text in one's own accents and gestures. In Russian, Bakhtin states, 'в отличие от внешне авторитарного слова слово внутренне убедительное в процессе его утверждающего усвоения тесно сплетается со «со своим словом'[1] (Bakhtin, 2012: 101). The translation from Russian to English is similar but not the same: the Russian words 'В отличие' (V otlichie) translated into English can mean 'unlike', 'difference', 'distinction', 'differentness' and/or 'otherness', but is often mistranslated as 'opposed' (Simpson & Dervin, 2017; Simpson, 2022). Internally persuasive discourse contains another[s] speech in one's own speech, meaning that internally persuasive discourse simultaneously struggles with existing ideologies and dogmatic viewpoints, whilst at the same time, it provides the possibility for discursive [re]accentuation and the diversifying of discursive meanings (Britzman, 2012). In the Russian language edition of his collection of essays, Bakhtin stresses that the boundaries between authoritative discourse and internally persuasive discourse are fluidly antagonistic (Simpson, 2018; Bakhtin, 2012).

Through a Bakhtin-Voloshinov approach to language (Simpson et al., 2020), I have argued that Bakhtin explicitly denies that the self can be understood in simple terms of self-identity – a human being never coincides with herself/himself (Simpson & Dervin, 2020; Simpson et al., 2022). The formula of identity 'A is A' is not applicable to a Bakhtinian approach for Interculturality (Simpson 2018; Simpson, 2022). For Bakhtin, the basis of being human (or human beings) is not self-identity but the opening of dialogue, an opening which always implies the simultaneous inter-animation of more than one voice (Simpson & Dervin, 2020). The voices contained within the self can be multiple and be ventriloquised when interacting with others, whereby the self can imitate multiple voices (Cooren & Sandler, 2014). In this sense, s/he may say they are gay or lesbian or bisexual, speak multiple languages, have multiple cultures, and so on (which may or may not be true), but whether these things are true or not is not the point Bakhtin is making here – these aspects of our being, are constantly in processes of becoming (Simpson & Dervin, 2020).

Pêcheux's work on ideology shows the subject cannot be considered as homogeneous as each society, each institution in society implies a certain way of legitimising speech, and particularly the kind of subject that is authorised to occupy a certain place (Maingueneau, 2011). This argument is akin to what the Sociologist Zygmunt Bauman in *Postmodernity and Its Discontents* (1997) calls the ordering zeal of the state characterised through legislated order of divisions, classifications, allocations and boundaries constructing the dividing lines between those that fit into society and those that do not, engendering the 'strangers' contra the 'familiar', 'us' versus 'them'. In this sense, the legitimising discursive function of the state (e.g. discourses such as the foreigner, the stranger, the outlier, the other) politicises (e.g. 'the migrant', 'the refugee' 'the asylum seeker') who is demarcated as a 'problem' (ibid.).

In this sense, the subject has become appropriated as something *other* than itself. In returning to the Munchausen Effect, Pêcheux argues:

> . . . each subject having really always-already begun – with the result that this question of the beginning as it were occults itself: this 'jumping in at the deep end', which is the specific form of the 'Munchausen effect' in the domain of the subjective appropriation of knowledges. (Pêcheux, 1982: 160)

To explain what Pêcheux means by the subjective appropriation of knowledges he gives the example of a child who is starting school and that there is never an educational starting point (the 'evident fact' that the child starts school at a specific temporal and spatial context does not necessarily mean that the child has started their education). Pêcheux argues that this example shows there are always pre-existent meanings to every discursive formation which have always-already begun (Pêcheux, 1982). These pre-existent meanings are constituted by the subject's relationality to wider societal forces and power relations. Thus, the speaking subject can never be conceptualised as the origin of their discourse. Neither can the utterances of an individual subject mark the origin of a specific discursive formation. Instead, in conceptualising the discursive construction of reality one needs to analyse how and why certain discourses were produced in the first place. In a sense, one needs to pay attention to the mediating forces that constantly metamorphosise the construction of discourse and language in our everyday lives.

To put this another way, in some forms of research on Interculturality the discourses of the speaking subject are often conceptualised as being exclusively the speakers' own, without paying attention to the interdiscursive or the dialogical construction of meaning-making. In this sense, the researchers' methodological approach can easily generalise and essentialise the speaker utterances as the speakers are presented as rational truth bearers whereby the speaking subject becomes the knowing subject (i.e. their utterances are taken as a form of objectivity in that the subject produces some form of knowledge) (Simpson, 2022). The rationalisations of the speaker utterances, as a speaking subject, totalise and negate the identities of the research participants found in the publications (which can paradoxically run contrary to the ideological and conceptual approach argued).

Self-identity is appropriated as something *other* than itself. Discourses do not simply coincide with one another (Pêcheux, 1982), nor do they illustrate a form of unified subjectivity found within the self (Bakhtin, 2012). Society has inherent contradictions that are expressed and performed within daily interactions between people.

The conceptualisation of Intercultural subject as the knowing subject reflects *the simulacrum of liberal interculturalist*, namely, an approach characterised through a displacement of images which focuses on the self as being rational and free, thus reflecting an extension of liberal modernity (see, Dervin & Simpson, 2021). These processes mark what I call the *biopolitics of everyday life* – the separation of the life of the person and the life of the animal (in a biological sense) characterised by the superiority of mind over body *through the absolute rationalisation of the speaking subject as the knowing subject* (Dervin & Simpson, 2021). This can be characterised through the plethora of initiatives whereby, through rationalism, Interculturality posits the self as needing to be competent in acquiring various skills, values or components of the Intercultural (for example see Byram, 2021; Deardorff, 2019; for models presented by Supranational Organisations see, Council of Europe, 2018; OECD 2018, UNESCO, 2013).

In applying Pêcheux's (1982) approach that the speaker never says what they mean then there is a conceptual paradox here for the rationality of the speaking subject. The problem lies in that one can never put oneself inside the mind of another to know what they are truly thinking and feeling or whether they are speaking on, or about, something which can be considered as being 'true'. To put this another way, the self could be deceiving the other in so far that they could be demonstrating a certain openness, tolerance or respect towards cultural differences (concepts found within a liberal framework of Intercultural Communicative Competence, for example, in Michael Byram's model [1997; 2021]) yet there is no real (or absolute) way of knowing what they are actually thinking or feeling about these particular values or principles (they could in fact be masquerading racist or discriminatory discourses). This conceptualisation of Interculturality merely reconstitutes the role of the self at the centre of such approaches and fails to adequately problematise how the self is constituted through continuous interactions with the other (Simpson et al., 2022; Simpson & Dervin, 2020). Though, such models like Byram's ICC (1997) model remain seductively appealing as they reinforce a certain phantasmic egocentricism that the self can become Interculturally competent or *be* Intercultural (whatever that means) without any way of validating such claims (as one can never transcend into the body or mind of another human being or 'know' what they are *really* feeling or experiencing).

In their publication, Adrian Holliday and Malcolm MacDonald (2020) raise similar issues in Intercultural research in terms of how interpretivist approaches to Interculturality can be problematic when the discourses of research participants are taken at 'face value'. However, where I disagree with Holliday and MacDonald lies in what they call 'recovering intersubjectivity'. Holliday & MacDonald (2020) advocate for a liquid conceptualisation of culture in line with Dervin (2011) and call for dialogue in terms of unearthing the discourses and ideologies which influence both researcher and research participant (in line with the overarching approach of reflexivity). Holliday and MacDonald, though, do not address the prediscursive ideological construction of the subject as noted by Pêcheux (1982) in that the subject in the research process, in a materialist sense, is already a subject of ideology. Firstly, the discursive origin of the subject is not, for example, the beginning of a dialogical interview or focus group on a subject matter within Interculturality (which is a mere snapshot), the subject already carries with it a mass constellation of differing ideologies and discourses before 'the moment of Interculturality'.

Secondly, Holliday and MacDonald argue for a liquid approach to culture which does not account for the Janusian (double-faced) functioning of discourses about the Intercultural (as Dervin also notes in his [2011] article). This means that one face of the subject may be posited towards reflexively engaging in the dialogue and constructing meanings with interlocutors, but the other faces of the subject may be posited elsewhere (as characterised by the many voices contained within one's speech), yet Holliday and MacDonald's pre-eminence on the rationality of both research participant and researcher can be problematic. To put this another way, as I articulate this through a Bakhtinian lens (Simpson, 2022) through the concept of outsideness (Bakhtin, 2012). 'Outsideness' (or *vnenakhodimost*) is understood as the intersubjective co-experience of an event of being (Brandist, 2002). The notion of 'outsideness' denotes the processes in which the self returns to her/his own position outside of the other in relation to the wholeness to what is being perceived (Brandist, 2002). The crisis of outsideness refers to the positions of self and the other in that there is 'no stable evaluative position from which a consistent outsideness can be maintained' (Brandist, 2002: 49). To put this simply, the self can never know absolutely what the other demands from it as one can never know what the other is thinking/feeling or how they have been constructed. Dialogues therefore consist of jumping into the deep end (to coin a phrase from Pêcheux) as one can never know with certainty what interlocutors will say or how their utterances have been influenced by prior discourses and to what extent the addressees' utterances function as mere lip service for what the other interlocutors want to hear (Bakhtin, 2012). In this sense, the discourses contained within reflexive co-constructed dialogues can still be interpreted and manipulated as something *other* than what is being represented, as these processes are still influenced and shaped by many ideologies and voices. In this sense, the self can be grappling with several different interdiscourses (shown through the refraction of the speakers' utterances) about Interculturality at a given time.

The final, and third aspect, relates to the subject-object relationship in Interculturality in terms of how the subject can be turned into an object. In focusing on neoliberalism, Holliday and MacDonald ahistoricise systematic processes and systems which mediate intercultural relations between people and between people and objects (Simpson & Dasli, 2023). They simply take a snapshot of neoliberalism instead of connecting the wider issues about othering and representation to a material basis. As a result, what Holliday and MacDonald propose does not prevent the speaking subject from turning their representations into objects (whereby an other *others* their self) through how they construct and transmit senses of belonging and identification. Therefore it is important to analyse the ways subjects orientate their utterances towards a superaddressee – 'various concrete ideological expressions' (Brandist, 2002: 169) whereby the interlocutor can 'never yield all of [*sic*] himself and all of his [*sic*] discursive work to the full and finalised will of present or nearby addressees' (Brandist, 2002). In this sense, in a co-constructed reflexive dialogue (or any dialogue for that matter) a speaker can still be orienting their utterances towards the ideological force of a superaddressee (see Blommaert, 2010). Every dialogue does not function in isolation as discourses come into being through the interplay of previous discourses (Maingueneau, 2011). Thus, it is important to pay attention to the interdiscursive social layers functioning within dialogues in order to problematise how subjects and objects are constructed through Interculturality. In this sense, intersubjectivity is not simply an event or object of research (i.e. a co-constructed dialogue), nor should it be assumed as being present merely because reflexive dialogues are taking place. As I show in the next sub-section, the relationship between Interculturality and intersubjectivity needs to be problematised in full and I do this in relation to the notion of community.

On the need to rethink representation through community

The notion of community has been discussed from many different perspectives and across disciplines, from anthropology, to sociology, psychology, and political theory, amongst others (e.g. Anderson, 2006; Bauman, 2001). The lexicon of community is often multifaceted and contradictory insofar that the notion cannot be translated into a political-philosophical endeavour (Esposito, 2009). Yet the same community is often reduced to 'an object' across discursive spaces and it is turned into 'a thing', a conceptual language which assumes the connotations of unity and commonality (Esposito, 2009). For Benedict Anderson (2006), communities are distinguished not by their falsity/genuineness but by 'the style in which they are imagined' (Anderson, 2006: 6). For Zygmunt Bauman (2001:71), the aesthetic of community can be described through the notion of peg communities – friable and short-lived bonds which are hung by a great number of individuals (like placing your coat on a peg then moving it and putting your coat on another peg). The notion of community is seemingly elusive, yet in research on Interculturality it is always assumed as being present (see Dervin, 2016); it always means something to someone, somewhere.

For the philosopher Roberto Esposito (2008; 2009; 2012; 2015; 2017), the relationship between subject and community is characterised by the negation of identity found in the subject. Esposito (2010; 2015) conceptualises community through the rupture of subjective identity rather than viewing community as an extension of the subject's identity. The latter (an extension of the subject's identity) is common in research on Interculturality as researchers often 'group' individual subjects in based on commonalities assumed from either the position of self or that of the other, for example, people may be grouped as 'migrant communities', 'linguistic communities' or 'cultural communities' as the specific target of particular Intercultural research, for Esposito though, community is instead understood as the subject's exposure to the loss of subjectivity (Esposito, 2015).

In *Communitas: Origin and Destiny of Community* (2010) Esposito argues, 'representation cannot represent itself but is always something other. This is how originary presence is already altered, decentered and separated from what it is. It is condemned to difference and therefore negated in its identity' (Esposito, 2009: 47).

The issue of representation is also taken up by Pêcheux whereby representation operates as if it were a concept, and simultaneously, the concept is reduced to pure representation (Pêcheux, 1982). In this sense, the object of the representation subsumes the subject as it negates the subject's subjectivity. Yet, community is not something that puts into relation what it is, it is (ontological) being itself as a relation (Esposito, 2015). Community is characterised by a disjuncture between a linguistic code that can be political only through reference to its subjects (as friendship or as enmity characterised by the engendering of 'us' versus 'them' discourses) and on the other hand that concerns 'being in common' as such (Esposito, 2015). Esposito articulates that community can no longer be thought of as a subjective bond (or objective bond) alone but 'rather as the space outlined by the impossibility of its operation' (Esposito, 2015: xxviii).

In this sense:

> In the community, subjects do not find a principle of identification nor an aseptic enclosure within which they can establish transparent communication or even a content to be communicated. They don't find anything else except that void, that distance, that extraneousness that constitutes them as being missing from themselves; 'givers to' inasmuch as they themselves are 'given by' a circuit of mutual gift giving that finds its own specificity in its indirectness with respect to the frontal nature of the subject-object relation or to the ontological fullness of the person (if not in the daunting semantic duplicity of the French *personne*, which can mean both 'person' and 'no one'). (Esposito, 2010: 7)

In seeming agreement with the philosopher Antonio Negri (2017) Esposito argues that Michel Foucault misguided the appropriation of the term *biopolitics*, Esposito argues that modern origins of biopolitics can be found in the immunising features of sovereignty, property and liberty in everyday life (Esposito, 2008). In *Communitas: Origin and Destiny of Community* (2009) Esposito problematises the relation between community and immunity, rather, than conceptualising the relationship as a juxtaposition, Esposito argues community and immunity can be understood as a move in which each term is inscribed reciprocally through the other (Esposito, 2008). In tracing the Latin etymology of the word *Communitas* Esposito argues that community is inhabited by the communal – *onus* and *officium* – concerns obligation and office, while the third paradoxically centres on *donum* – a gift that combines *onus* and *officium* – obligation and office (Esposito, 2008). Communitas thus demands an exchange – a gift – in return. This gift is continuous and always vis-à-vis the other (ibid.). Thus,

> thinking community through *communitas* will name the gift that keeps on giving, a reciprocity in the gift that doesn't, indeed cannot, belong to oneself. At its (missing) origin, *communitas* is constructed around an absent gift, one that members of the community cannot keep for themselves. (Esposito, 2008: x)

Thus, communities are inherently defective, the effects of reciprocal donation on individual identity mean that accepting the *munus* [duty or gift] the individual undermines their efforts to identify herself/himself as such, in order to 'be part of a community' the subject loses part of its subjectivity (Esposito, 2010). In this sense, the community isn't a mode of being, neither is it a making of individual subjects, nor is it an extension or multiplication of their subjectivities, rather, what the community interrupts, it turns inside out: 'a dizziness, a syncope, a spasm in the continuity of the subject' (Esposito, 2010: 7). This continuity of the subject leads to the swelling of the self, whereby 'intersubjectivity always intent on finding otherness in an alter ego similar in everything to the *ipse* [self] that they would like to challenge and that instead they reproduce' (Esposito, 2010: 2). The problematique here is precisely one of totality, 'the representative doubling of its presence and the essentialisation of its existence' (Esposito, 2010: 15). Esposito argues that community functions by enclosing the subject, the subject's essence becomes essentialised through an exteriorisation of their being, in a sense the subject essentialises its own identity.

Historically, Interculturally has been founded upon assumptions about what individual and group representations may mean or what they *are* (See Dervin, 2016). Often community is presented and represented as an 'objective fact' or a given reality (presented in the singular and discursively imposed from the position of the speaking subject as 'a given' or imposed by researchers onto the subjects of their inquiry). This conceptualisation of community seemingly evades questions surrounding the type and form of community the subject belongs to or what constitutes given communities in the first instance – whether this be about research on Interculturality focusing on commonalities found in social groups (for example, migrants, newcomers, refugees, asylum seekers) or in how Interculturality can be part of and/or facilitate the emergence of supranational level initiatives (e.g. ideologies which promote the notion of the global community, global citizenry, cosmopolitanism, internationalisation, and so on).

This problematique raises issues for the historical conceptualisation of Intercultural Communication research. From Edward T. Hall's ((1959) high and low-order cultural contexts, to Geert Hofstede's (1983) dichotomy of collectivist and individualist cultures/countries, to Michael Byram's (1997) emphasis on national culture and of culture being a synonym for country (my words), to cosmopolitan approaches such as Adrian Holliday's (2016) small culture and big culture formation, the red thread that unites these approaches is the misconceptualisation of what people have *in common* and what *unites* people. The *common* is often misconceptualised though empiricist and essentialist apparatuses (e.g. through normative static concepts such as 'culture', 'objective truths' about people and their environments, and the fact that the speaking subject is always presented as being rational and free, i.e. sovereign over 'their Interculturality') in terms of determining what people associate to, what they belong to, or what they identify as/towards. This understanding of *the common* as an extension of the subject's identity runs contrary to Esposito's theoretical conceptualisations (Esposito, 2008; 2010; 2015).

Historical Intercultural Communication models and the research which has followed have emasculated the identity of the subject by essentialising its presence and essence in relation to what is assumed the subject belongs to (impositions from the speaking subject or by researchers onto the subjects of their inquiry). Whether that be so-called identifiable groups of people due to predetermined and politicised statuses inscribed by state apparatuses such as refugees, migrants and asylum seekers (Bauman, 1997), or, whether that be through generalisations about the subject's subjectivity, for example, that a group of people share commonalities based on their language (e.g. target language group), culture, national identity or by other intersectional markers (such as age, race, gender, religion and so on). Research in the field thus has inherently assumed what *the common* entails, or put simply, the field has (falsely) assumed what *unites* people (and conversely what divides people e.g. through the pre-occupation with culturalism in Interculturality [Dervin & Simpson, 2021]). Researchers, who may have 'good intentions' (e.g. in the work of non-essentialist [Huang, 2021] or decolonial [Guilherme, 2019] approaches) in their research on Interculturality in terms of fighting for a particular issue or cause in the name of social justice can fall into the trap of assuming that particular commonalities exist in the construction of social groups and group identities. As Esposito reminds us, communities can

> no longer be conceived as a product of shared will, nor as the line of death that subjects join in a kind of sacrificial ecstasy, because it precedes every will and every subject as the originary *munus* [duty/gift[2]] from which they arise as an uninterrupted expropriation. (Esposito, 2015: xxix)

In this sense, what unites subjects to community is their loss of subjectivity not a form of self-identity (i.e. what the self identifies as).

At this juncture, it is important to clarify to the reader that the philosophy of Roberto Esposito is not founded upon negative philosophy or negation (e.g. in what can be found in the work of Hegel). In *Bios: Biopolitics and Philosophy* (2008) Esposito sketches out his interpretation of biopolitics as somewhere 'in-between' (Esposito, 2008: viii) Giorgio Agamben's (2017) negative interpretation of biopolitics and its separation of bare life *(zoē)* from political forms of life *(bios)*, and Antonio Negri's (2017) positive interpretation of biopolitics as multitude. *In Interculturality and the Political* I sketch out my own interpretation of Esposito's work in relation to Interculturality which is characterised by a section of the book I call the 'Biopolitics of Interculturality' (Dervin & Simpson, 2021) in which I argue the systemic societal apparatus of Interculturality functions as (biological) racial differences as cultural/linguistic differences through the simulacrum of the liberal interculturalist. When thinking about how the concept of culture (and cultural difference) is used in research on Interculturality and how this has been rationalised for decades, Espositoargues, 'culture de-solidarises, if it erects barriers and constructs genres, if it defines gradations in the participation in the notion of humanity, tracing horrible borders between "us" and "the barbarians" ' (Esposito, 2020 in Dervin & Simpson, 2021: 99).

At the heart of this thesis lies the necessity to move beyond simplistic descriptions of what differentiates and to instead problematise whether the *commons* can be problematised for Interculturality. Esposito articulates *the common* as:

> The common is not characterized by what is proper but by what is improper, or even more drastically, by the other; by a voiding [*svuotamento*], be it partial or whole, of property into its negative; by removing what is properly one's own [*depropriazwne*] that invests and decenters the proprietary subject, forcing him to take leave [*uscire*] of himself, to alter himself. (Esposito, 2009: 7)

One of the purposes of this book, in line with Esposito's thought, is to problematise what *the common* might mean in developing a dialectical perspective for research on Interculturality. As xenophobia, racism, inequalities and fractures in our societies become more and more visible (I am not suggesting they were previously invisible) the final chapters of this book are dedicated to conceptualising a dialectical approach for Interculturality by arguing for a form of Interculturality which is underpinned by problematising what solidarises our experiences as human beings.

Structure of this book

Following on from this introduction where the scene has been set in terms of the positioning of the book in relation to research on Interculturality and the key arguments have been presented. The next chapter of the book focuses on exploring the relationship between the speaking subject in Interculturality and the Munchausen Effect and will problematise whether it is possible to go beyond the primacy of the speaking subject in research on Interculturality. The Munchausen Effect in Interculturality is critiqued through a conceptual analysis based upon Michel Pêcheux's work on ideology and by bringing in dialectical perspectives from Marxism and critical realism.

The third chapter deals with the problem of the subject-object relationship in research on Interculturality. The Munchausen Effect, which is conceptualised in the previous chapter, is critiqued in relation to questions of representation in Interculturality. Namely, this chapter offers a dialectical engagement with Marxian and critical realism thought in advocating for an approach to discourse and representation which includes both language and materiality. The approach presented is positioned as conceptual intervention to move Interculturality beyond the Munchausen Effect.

In the fourth chapter I elaborate on a dialectical approach for Interculturality. In doing so, I engage with Marxian and critical realist texts to decipher the dialectical within Interculturality. Central to this argument is an engagement with language, culture and community as functioning as commodity-like social relations. I argue that a critical engagement with the notion of community is vital in order shifting Interculturality conceptually beyond egocentric and phonocentric approaches found within the field.

The fifth chapter discusses what people have in common in Interculturality in problematising questions surrounding what the commons might mean for Interculturality. In building on the dialectical perspective presented I have presented in earlier chapters I argue that the focus for Interculturality should be on acknowledging and interrogating relations of alienation-disalienation within the commons. I argue that if Interculturality is serious about being a form of critical praxis in relation to issues of social justice then understanding the production and reproduction of societal alienation-disalienation is essential.

The final chapter, which is the concluding chapter, looks back at the discussions from the previous chapters and proposes in teasing out the implications of my dialectical argument for current and future scholarship on Interculturality. In doing so, I reaffirm how a dialectical approach for Interculturality can overcome the conceptual symptoms of the Munchausen Effect.

Notes

1 'Unlike externally authoritative discourse, internally persuasive discourse whilst in the process of its affirmative assimilation is tightly intertwined with "one's own word" ' (my translation).

2 My words.

2 Interculturality and the Problem of the Speaking Subject

The problematique of the speaking subject

In analysing the conceptual and practical roles of the speaking subject in relation to Interculturality one must first problematise the speaking subject conceptually through an engagement with wider theories of language and of language use. In doing so, I will trace and map the problems associated with the speaking subject – provocatively, however, I will propose whether these 'problems' are problems which are exclusive of 'the speaking subject', or whether these 'problems' relate to all subjects. These issues will be elucidated in this chapter and subsequent chapters of the book.

In conceptually approaching and problematising the speaking subject, in *Reflections on Exile and Other Literary and Cultural Essays* Edward Said (2001) argues that '[Edmund] Husserl passed to the belief that one's concern ought to be "the speaking subject", since there is no such thing as a language that one does not use' (Said, 2001:10). For Said, language is used and, in a word, performed, in which one expresses meanings about facets found within one's daily life – a reflection of, how one understands, life.

Said (2001:12) goes on to articulate:

> Spoken language is only one of a series of concentric circles that surround Man [*sic*] in society, for kinship systems, mythology (as Barthes and Levi-Strauss have shown), political ideas, even household objects are varieties of human expression that correspond to each other and to language.

DOI: 10.4324/9781003283713-2

In these sections of *Reflections on Exile and Other Literary and Cultural Essays*, Said (2001) sketches out the poststructuralist oeuvre of language function and use insofar that language, discursively speaking, permeates within both subjects and objects, and gives meaning to socially constructed realities. Yet, the meanings associated with objects, i.e. 'things' and people, for Said, are inherently polysemic and unstable. Said (2001), quoting Maurice Merleau-Ponty in *Sense and Non-sense* (1964), articulates that language surrounds the speaking subject

> like an instrument with its own inertia, its own demands, constrains, and internal logic, it must nevertheless remain open to the initiatives of the subject, always capable of the displacement of meanings, the ambiguities, and the functional substitutions which give this logic its lurching gait. (Said, 2001: 11)

Said goes onto argue that the poststructuralist approaches of Michel Foucault and Francois Lyotard mean that the 'great narratives of emancipation and enlightenment are over' (Said, 2001: 244). From a materialist and dialectical perspective this quotation is incredibly worrisome and in later chapters of the book will explicitly discuss struggles for social justice in relation to concepts such as alienation. Whether or not Said intended for this statement to be interpreted literally one might not know, but certainly what Said argues next can be contested:

> . . . but I think what we must remember more seriously what Foucault himself teaches, that in this case, as in many others, it is sometimes of paramount importance not so much *what* is said, but *who* speaks. (Said, 2001: 244)

Here, it seems that Said is somewhat passively, acknowledging or perhaps even reproducing what Jacques Derrida has called phonocentrism – namely, 'phonocentrism-logocentrism relates to centrism itself – the human desire to posit a "central" presence at beginning and end' (Derrida, 1997: lxviii). Said seemingly reproduces the logics of egocentrism and self-centrism which are placed at the heart of phonocentrism – 'I say that I am X therefore I am X' – this is an unquestionable normative truth which cannot be disputed. Said's preoccupation with who speaks over what is said arguably reproduces the privileging of speech over writing which is central to Derrida's (1997) thinking in *Of Grammatology*. In essence, Said does not adequately grapple with the problem of the speaking subject and how the speech of the speaking subject can reproduce dogmatic thinking. Derrida (1997) articulates that

> this notion [of the signifier and the signified] remains therefore within the heritage of that logocentrism which is also a phonocentrism: absolute proximity of voice and being, of voice and the meaning of being, of voice and the ideality of meaning. (Derrida, 1997: 11–12)

For Derrida the phonocentric subject is ultimately an egocentric subject whose being, like language, is constituted by an infinite number of endless signifiers (Derrida, 1997). Yet, constructions of phonocentrism must be considered as being constructed by wider social and historical processes. In *Global English and Political Economy* John O'Regan articulates phonocentrism in late capitalism as: 'it [language] is being transformed through the discursive valorisation of language as speech' (O'Regan, 2021: 202). Whereby, the phonocentrism of language functions as a 'site of essence, oneness and truth' (O'Regan, 2021: 203). O'Regan here identifies some of the conceptual problems associated with poststructuralism insofar that the shift (or turn) to the discursive has invariably led to the reassertion of the individual, of the self, over the systemic or the structural – in essence, a reassertion of the centrism of the speaking subject (see also [Block, 2017] on the conceptual challenges of bringing discussions on political economy into applied linguistics research), in the sense that the utterances spoken by an individual must be accepted as a universal truth – marking the 'end' of a totalised process. In order to move beyond or break from the centrism of the speaking subject I propose that one considers the speaking subject from the position of wider systematic and structural forces. In doing so I argue for an engagement with the work of Michel Pêcheux.

The interpellation of the speaking subject

For Michel Pêcheux (1982), in laying the foundations of what Pêcheux calls 'a materialist theory of discourse' (Pêcheux, 1982: 97), Pêcheux argues for a focus on language through analysing the ideological conditions of societal reproduction and of the relations of the means of production which cannot ignore the economic conditions and factors which influence ideological apparatuses (Pêcheux, 1982). In this sense, Pêcheux is drawing on inspiration from Louis Althusser's ([1971] 2014) *On the Reproduction of Capitalism: Ideology and Ideological State Apparatuses*. For Pêcheux, ideologies have a productive function insofar that they should be seen as a practice (Pêcheux, 1982). These productive forces construct the properties by which rules are structured and ordered. Althusser (2014: 51) argues that such rules are structured by class, whereby, if one takes the example of language, students at school are told to 'speak properly', 'write properly' and 'talk properly'. For Althusser, the submission to these rules marks 'labour-power's submission to the dominant ideology' (Althusser, 2014: 51). Pêcheux, extends and builds upon Althusser's discussions by arguing that 'ideological apparatuses are not pure instruments of the ruling class' (Pêcheux, 1982: 98) – thus, ideologies do not necessarily reproduce a certain notion or idea, rather, they reproduce the existing social relations of society, namely, capitalist political economy. Like relations of capitalism which construct and engender contradictions, injustices and inequalities, the productive function of ideologies means that ideologies (like those of capitalism) can be characterised by their inherent unevenness (Pêcheux, 1982). In this sense, the nexus of knowledge, ideologies and language cannot be divorced from capitalist modes of production – they are produced within thecapitalist mode of production. The unevenness of capitalism constructs what Pêcheux (1982: 99) calls 'unevenness-subordination' – the division of ideological objects (e.g., knowledge, family, ethics, etc.) which compete as separate moments (i.e. elements) against one another.

At this juncture, Pêcheux (1982: 103) differentiates between Ideology and ideology (n.b. note the uppercase 'I' and the lowercase 'i'), whereby the former (i.e. Ideology) has 'in general no history' and the latter (i.e. ideology) denotes 'a concrete historical existence' which has been constructed through unevenness, contradiction and subordination. In this sense, subject-to-subject relations and how subjects are constituted can be understood through a process of interpellation – that the subject is a 'self-evident fact' (Althusser, 2014: 189) whereby 'ideology hails or interpellates concrete individuals as concrete subjects' (Althusser, 2014: 190). For example, as a subject I exist in reality – this is real and undisputable. For Althusser (2014: 192) the subject is '*always-already*' a subject meaning that ideology pre-exists the subject – Althusser (2014: 192–193) gives the example of how an unborn child exhibits ideologies about e.g., identity and sexuality before the child is born. However, Pêcheux (1982: 106) offers an alternative reading of the interpellation of the subject, firstly, when the subject says 'I speak' it needs to be considered that the subject is spoken *of* and the subject is spoken *to* before speaking. Therefore, the subject as an interpellated subject needs to be viewed through a wider enunciative process (Pêcheux, 1982). The second aspect Pêcheux (1982) takes issue with relates to the ideological stamp Althusser's interpellation attaches to the pre-existing subject whereby a sense of collective identity is imposed upon the individual. Pêcheux argues that the process of interpellation-identification is not simply the meaning attributed to something or the meaning imposed onto a subject, rather, interpellation-identification should be viewed as a process of 'what represents the subject for another signifier' (Pêcheux, 1982: 106). For Pêcheux (1982) one needs to problematise how subjects are ideologically constituted through wider social processes and power relations. This movement involves questioning 'how all individuals accept as evident the meaning of what they hear and say, and read and write as speaking subjects' (Pêcheux, 1982: 109). A failure to question the speaking subject can reproduce the Munchausen Effect 'by positing the subject as the origin of the subject, i.e. in what concerns us, by positing the subject of discourse as the origin of the subject of discourse (Pêcheux, 1982: 109)'.

Pêcheux makes this argument to move beyond what he calls metaphysical fantasies about the subject, in the sense that if the subject is posited as the origin of the subject and the origin of the subject of discourse then both the knowledge about the subject and the discursive acts themselves cannot be solely attributed to, and constitutive of, an individual subject (Pêcheux, 1982). Instead, the speaking subject and their discourses needs to be considered as an ongoing social process between people which is mediated by social forces and systems. To put this another way, the speaking subject, as a subject of enunciation cannot take up a position as a subject with 'full awareness, of the consequences of complete responsibility, [with] total freedom' (Pêcheux, 1982: 156). If one assumes and generalises that the subject has complete awareness of the consequences of complete responsibility with total freedom then one becomes subjugated to the word of the speaking subject – then one is besotted blindly to the memory of Baron Munchausen, who lifted himself up into the air by pulling his own hair. Pêcheux (1982) brings us to consider the important questions: How does ideology recruit individuals? And importantly, why does ideology recruit individuals? Instead of viewing the subject as a universal knowing subject (see Simpson, 2022) Pêcheux brings us to question the evident meanings surrounding what one hears and says, and what is read and written. This thinking seemingly resonates with aspects of Mikhail Bakhtin's (2012) work on dialogism and the wider oeuvre of The Bakhtin Circle e.g., Valentin Voloshinov's (1973) work on *Marxism and the Philosophy of Language*. In this sense, language should be viewed in relation to the subject as something which is inherently refracted by social relations, processes and forces. Language contains multiple layers of meaning which are ideologically posited in constructing contradictory and uneven social realities, realities which in turn, (re)produce material relations within society. These social realties cannot be divorced from the productive system of forces which they have been constructed by and within – namely, capitalism. In line with William Simpson and John O'Regan (2018: 155–156), I agree, therefore, that language itself cannot be articulated as a fetishised form of commodification as language appears as a commodity but it is not explicitly a product of labour (see also Block, 2014). As Simpson and O'Regan (2018: 164) conclude, 'it is the essential nature of capitalism that value lies in the processes of production of commodities, rather than in their physical character or in the human desire for them'. I will continue this discussion on commodity fetishism in the subsequent sections of this book when bringing the notion of community to the fore. For now, though, I will problematise the Munchausen Effect of the speaking subject in relation to Interculturality through a wider conceptual engagement.

Interculturality and the philosophical discourse of modernity

Interculturality is inherently phonocentric as a field and discipline. This is due to the egocentric position attributed to the speaking subject in the field. This position must be contextualised, though, from within the wider apparatus of the global political economy, whereby the hegemonic role of English language has dominated foreign language teaching and learning (O'Regan, 2021). Within Intercultural Communication more specifically, the Munchausen Effect can perhaps be best evidenced by the notion of the intercultural speaker (see Byram, 2008). The notion of the intercultural speaker is conceptualised through the assessment of socio-cultural competencies, many of which are derived from Michael Byram's (1997) Intercultural Communicative Competence model.

Byram conceptualises the intercultural speaker as having the ability 'to see relationships between different cultures – both internal and external to a society – and to mediate, that is interpret each in terms of the other, either for [himself] or for other people' (Byram, 2000: 10). Byram, assumes that the self has an awareness of both itself, the other and the material contexts in which both self and other are contextually determined. Moreover, mediation and interpretation here denote a politics of interaction underpinned by respect and tolerance – whereby, interaction can lead to the erasure of all differences (MacDonald & O'Regan, 2013; Hoff, 2014; Ferri, 2018; Dasli & Simpson, 2023). Here, in interaction, liberalised ideologies of preventing conflict or (intercultural) communication mishaps prevail over the necessity for debate and contestation (Dervin & Simpson, 2021). Central to Byram's notion of the intercultural speaker is the view that 'acting interculturally is to bring into a relationship two cultures' (Byram, 2008: 68). Yet, in earlier sections of his work, in relation to a group of Italian immigrants, Byram (2008) problematises the rather reductive and binary question: 'Do you feel Belgian or [are you] still Italian?' (Byram, 2008: 63). Here, culture is conceptualised as a normative fixed entity in the sense that culture is either one thing or another, a binary juxtaposition, demarcated by culture functioning as a synonym, for and of, nationality.

The problem with how Byram and other Interculturalists have posited the speaking subject in Intercultural Communication is that the subject in interaction is constructed as the origin of their discourse, the origin of their self. This subject seemingly does not pre-exist before their spoken act or exist after the act. For example, Hild Hoff's (2014) criticisms of Byram's ICC model and of the intercultural speaker (Hoff, 2016) are important considerations in thinking about how conflict, misunderstandings and disagreements shape intercultural interactions. At this juncture, it is important to note that Intercultural Communication has historically been constructed through empiricist logics and practices which have exclusively focused on interactions in the here and now (Ferri, 2018; 2023). In other publications, I have argued that the prevailing modernist rationalisation of self-centric discourses results in an over-spill of the self in Intercultural Communication research whereby the authorial position and depositions about the self seemingly cannot be questioned

(Simpson, 2022). Indeed, the Munchausen Effect is liberal egocentrism par excellence – insofar that the self becomes infatuated by its own fantasies about its selfhood. Therefore, rather than seeing the development of postmodernist and poststructuralist approaches in the social sciences, as noted by the discursive turn attributed in Intercultural Communication (see Dasli & Diaz, 2017), as a break with and from modernity, one must rethink this insofar that the discursive turn can lead to the extension of (rather than the break from or rupture from) modernity (Simpson & Dasli, 2023).

In elucidating this argument further an engagement with the dialectics of critical realism might be important for whether language and Intercultural Communication can break from postmodernist approaches (see e.g., Block, 2013). In drawing on the critical realist philosopher Margret Archer (1995; 2000; 2010), David Block (2013) argues that the historical debate of structure versus agency has been constructed as a false binary relation (my interpretation), whereby some sociological approaches found within post and late modernity have privileged agency over structure (e.g., Giddens, 2000). Instead, through an engagement with Archer and the French sociologist Pierre Bourdieu (2003; 2004), Block (2013) questions whether research participants are morphostatic or morphogenetic – namely, whether they reproduce or transform existing socio-cultural orders. This argument raises important considerations in terms of the importance of combining both structure and agency (rather than seeing these notions in opposition) together in problematising social activity in language and Intercultural Communication. Thus, as characteristics of the Munchausen Effect, phonocentrism and egocentrism must be viewed as being historically and socially contextual. As Karl Marx reminds us, ‘it is our social being that determines our consciousness and not the other way round’ (Marx, 1976: 3; O’Regan 2021: 20). This, therefore, ‘leaves room for agency [and structure]’ (O’Regan, 2021: 7).

In taking this discussion forward, the Munchausen Effect must be, therefore, discussed as a characteristic and symptom emerging from the production of capitalist societies. The Philosophical Discourse of Modernity (PDM) as articulated by the critical realist philosopher Roy Bhaskar (2002; 2016; 2020), is ‘a very pure ideology of the capitalist mode of production’ (Bhaskar, 2002: 64). In engaging with Marx’s *Capital Vol. 1.* (1990) for Bhaskar PDM ‘obtains at the level of the real’ (Hartwig, 2011: 486) and ‘operates in tandem with capital accumulation as an implicit structuring mechanism' (O'Regan, 2022: 6). Bhaskar's critique of Jürgen Habermas' (1987) *The Philosophical Discourse of Modernity* can perhaps be best conceptualised in his (2016) book *Enlightened Common Sense: The Philosophy of Critical Realism*. In the book, Bhaskar argues that PDM is an epistemic fallacy which prioritises epistemology over ontology and 'thought over body, emotion and spirit' (Bhaskar, 2016: 177). In line with the egocentrism of the speaking subject which has been discussed earlier in this chapter, for Bhaskar, PDM is conceptualised upon a false assumption of the 'I' which prioritises the individual over others in society (Bhaskar, 2016). Bhaskar, therefore, rejects the Cartesian *cogito ergo sum*: I think therefore I am. In doing so, Bhaskar argues that in this sense, the prioritisation of 'I' over others in society produces atomistic ego-centricity – 'a persistent model of the human being as propertied as tacitly gendered as male' (Bhaskar, 2016: 180). Another aspect linked to the egocentric positioning of the subject within PDM is the notion of disenchantment 'in the discourse of modernity from the outset, whereby the world was intrinsically drained of intrinsic meaning and value, which were sourced instead to the self-defining modern subject' (Bhaskar, 2016: 182).

It is probably not a surprise to the reader that Bhaskar is equally as critical of approaches found within postmodernism and poststructuralism which are seen as being grounded within PDM. For Bhaskar, postmodernism is seen as an extension of modernity which can be characterised by the conceptualisation of self as ego (Bhaskar, 2020). Bhaskar argues that PDM has produced an 'unholy trinity of irrealism' (Bhaskar, 2016: 183) which can be characterised by the epistemic fallacy (a reduction of reality to our knowledge about reality), ontological monovalence (the view that being is purely positive) and actualism (the notion that people are always the same at all times and in all places). Bhaskar (2016: 183) argues that fundamentalism is a cousin of postmodernism (and vice versa). For Bhaskar, 'like postmodernism, fundamentalism rejects universality and unity and accepts the essentiality of difference', but says, 'I'm right and you're wrong' to postmodernism's 'there is no right and wrong' (Bhaskar, 2016: 183). For Bhaskar, the problem of judgmental relativism is exacerbated by postmodernism and poststructuralism where the epistemic fallacy (e.g., the reduction of reality to our knowledge about reality) takes a 'linguistic form' (Bhaskar, 2016: 193) producing, what Bhaskar calls, ontological irrealism and judgemental irrationalism.

For Bhaskar, in postmodernist and poststructuralist approaches 'difference is emphasised at the cost of an understanding of structure and change' (Bhaskar, 2016: 197).

So, what does this mean for Interculturality? At a time when more and more voices within the field are calling for epistemological plurality within Intercultural Communication (see e.g., R'boul, 2021; 2022a), Bhaskar, and other critical realist scholars, remind us that conceptually agency and structure must be combined to move beyond epistemic fallacies about knowledge production and reproduction (see e.g., Block, 2013). The problematique, here, is that interpretivist epistemologies found within postmodernist and poststructuralist approaches can reproduce the PDM by failing to acknowledge and analyse the conditions (e.g., structures and systems) which (re)produce society, namely capitalist political economy. In doing so the epistemic fallacy, the reduction of reality to our knowledge about reality, is continually reproduced within Interculturality in linguistic form, i.e. through the exclusive status given to the discourses of the subject. As a symptom, the problem of the Munchausen Effect brings forward implications for questions of agency within Interculturality. If the Munchausen Effect in Interculturality means that phonocentrism and egocentrism of the speaking subject seemingly cannot be questioned, then how does one adequately problematise injustices and inequalities in relation to agency? Later sections of this book will deal with this question which I shall come back to. However, for Bhaskar, PDM produces ontological monovalence, 'the irrealist problematic resonate with the social problems of generalised master–slave-type relations' (Bhaskar, 2016: 187). In this sense, power relations are seen as a point of continuity rather than discontinuity; they are not 'giving agency' to a subject, on the contrary, they reproduce prevailing systems and structures. In this sense, power relations continue the processes of structuring and ordering the prevailing system (Norrie, 2010). This discussion is a warning towards calls for epistemological pluralism and diversity in Interculturality, insofar that Intercultural epistemologies have histories that have emerged and been produced from within the same historical systems and structures which they are now meant to be correcting in relation to issues of social justice. In this sense, contesting issues of social justice in Interculturality needs to be connected to wider materialist dynamics in historicising real-life situations and experiences (in analysing the influences and factors of how these real-life situations and experiences are produced and reproduced). In later chapters of this book, I will continue to explore this discussion further by problematising how capitalist political economy influences and mediates both language and Interculturality.

Synopsis: Interculturality beyond the speaking subject?

To summarise, this chapter has discussed the following:

- The problem of the speaking subject in Interculturality can be characterised by the phenomenon of the Munchausen Effect.
- The Munchausen Effect can be characterised by phonocentrism (the privileging of the spoken word over the written word) and by egocentrism (the privileging of the 'I' – which Roy Bhaskar (2016) refers to in reproducing the epistemic fallacy – the reduction of reality to our knowledge about reality).
- As discussed in relation to the critical discourse work of Pêcheux (1982), in attempting to break with, or from, the egocentric fantasies of the speaking subject one must consider a materialist theory of discourse. An approach which analytically brings both structure and agency and epistemology and ontology together within the wider dynamics of applied linguistics research (see e.g., Block, 2013; 2017).
- In drawing on the critical realist approaches of Roy Bhaskar (2016; 2020) amongst others, the Munchausen Effect can be conceptualised as being a symptom of the Philosophical Discourse of Modernity (PDM).
- Here, PDM is both structured and ordered by the political economy of capitalism. This ordering and structuring is achieved through capitalist modes of production and through the conceptualisation of self as ego (Bhaskar, 2020).
- Interculturality is, therefore, inherently egocentric and phonocentric in its conceptual positioning. Rather, than seeing postmodernist and poststructuralist turns in the field as being 'critical' turns in Intercultural Communication, the dominant PDM in Interculturality means that postmodernist and poststructuralist approaches have led to an extension of the subject of modernity (through hyper relativity), rather, than a break from the subject of modernity. In this

sense, Interculturality remains an inherently modernist and positivist endeavour.

In moving this discussion forward, in the next chapter I will continue to problematise Interculturality and the Munchausen Effect. I do so by discussing how representation is produced and reproduced in Interculturality.

3 Interculturality, Representation and the Munchausen Effect

The problem of representation and the Munchausen Effect

In the previous chapter of this book I unpacked the problem of the Munchausen Effect and how this can be traced through language and society. In doing so, I conceptually critiqued the phonocentric and egocentric foundation of Interculturality from a dialectical perspective which views these phenomena through the lens of the Philosophical Discourse of Modernity (PDM). Of course, though, the issues surrounding the egocentric and phonocentric speaking subject cannot be viewed in isolation. Nor can their effects be viewed as being unidimensional. Whether someone, somewhere, refers to themselves as X or Y, or whether someone *other* attributes this meaning to them, is not the point here, precisely, this brings forth the issue of representation and the construction of the relation between representation and meaning. To put this simply, the problematique that we are dealing with here is how one attributes meaning to 'things' through acts of representation and whether it is possible to refrain from falling into the Munchausen Effect. In problematising this further, this chapter of the book focuses on mapping the historical and social relations of representation before mapping out a dialectical perspective for representation.

Acknowledging the Munchausen Effect in Interculturality means acknowledging the social and historical constructions of reality. The symptomatic fantasies of the Munchausen Effect can be traced through the PDM and through the dominant productive forces of society, namely capitalist political economy. In moving towards a critical realist perspective, methodologically one must first engage with

DOI: 10.4324/9781003283713-3

Marxian works in moving towards the Critical Realist dialectic, it is therefore no surprise that Roy Bhaskar notes that Karl Marx 'himself was in important ways implicitly a critical realist *avant la lettre*' (Singh et al., 2020: 237).

At this juncture, I feel it is necessary to clarify to the reader why the following paragraphs of this section follow an engagement with Marxian texts. Firstly, this is a necessary conceptual engagement in order to lay the foundations of what will be discussed in later sections of this chapter, and in later chapters of this book, in relation to developing a dialectical perspective for Interculturality. Secondly, in critiquing the Munchausen Effect in Interculturality, as the previous chapters have delineated, it is necessary to bring together an analytic including both structures and systems in critiquing the phonocentrism and egocentrism of the speaking subject. Thirdly, if the field is truly interdisciplinary it is necessary to engage in different theories and approaches from across the social sciences in problematising whether it is possible to 'make sense of Interculturality'. Fourthly (it was not my intention to write these aspects as a reductive list but it might help in showing my logic), it is important to acknowledge the impact of reading Marx's works by philosophers and theorists who have influenced both language and Interculturality (in the broad sense), which may include, but is not exclusive of, scholars such as Stuart Hall, Michel Foucault, Edward Said, Pierre Bourdieu, Chantal Mouffe, Walter Mignolo, Jacques Derrida and Judith Butler, to name but a few.

Firstly, a few preliminary thoughts before engaging with some aspects of Marx's works. It is important to acknowledge, as David Harvey (2023) comments in his recent book *A Companion to Marx's Grundrisse*, that there have been deliberate misrepresentations and false representations of Marx's writings, which means that it is impossible to read Marx from an uncluttered perspective. For example, the way Marx wrote *Grundrisse: Foundations of the Critique of Political Economy* (1993), which was written in the style of notes (often to himself), means that many of the notions and ideas are elusive (Harvey, 2023). Indeed, the conceptualisation of Marx's analysis takes the reader in many divergent directions and should be read as such (Harvey, 2012; 2023). Indeed, it is important to note that in *The Limits to Capital* David Harvey argues that Marx's works should be viewed as incomplete fragments (Harvey, 2018b) – a starting point for introspection and for further critique. I am also aware of recent debates calling for new translations of Marx's works in relation to the Anglophone dominance of translations of Marx's works, notwithstanding, translation inaccuracies arising from translating Marx's works from German into English (Haug, 2017). Nonetheless, this brings us to Marx's dialectical method.

In *A Companion to Marx's Capital: The Complete Edition*, Harvey (2018a) shows 'Marx never wrote a tract on dialectics' (Harvey, 2018a: 14), yet often Marx's dialectical method has been misinterpreted or misunderstood (Harvey, 2018a). Central to this misunderstanding, for Harvey, is the notion that Marx is 'some sort of fixed and immovable structuralist thinker' (Harvey, 2018a: 14). Whereas, for Harvey and for Henri Lefebvre (2014), Marx's analytic captured the constant fluidity and dynamism of society and of the social relations mediated by capitalism – forces which constantly engender the social fabric of everyday life (Lefebvre, 2014). This social fabric of everyday life includes peoples, languages and their identities – that are all in a constant process of becoming. Harvey reaffirms this argument through the following passage:

> What Marx seeks out in *Capital* is a concrete apparatus, a deep structure, that explains the way in which motion is actually instantiated within a capitalist mode of production. Consequently, many of his concepts are formulated around *relations* rather than stand-alone principles; they are about transformative activity. (Harvey, 2018a: 15)

Indeed, it may (or may not) surprise the reader that Harvey goes on to call Marx's intervention in the 1850s a 'deconstruction' (Harvey, 2018a: 16) of nineteenth-century political economy. In his work *Marx's Notes on Method* Stuart Hall (2003) argues that Marx's critique of the ideological presupposition of political economy, in differing from the classical liberal approaches, argues 'the individual [producer] cannot be the point of departure, but only *the result*' (Hall, 2003: 115). For Marx, the liberal approaches of philosophers such as Jean-Jacques Rousseau and the like, strip the subject away from the materialist complexities which produce and shape society. Marx (1993) in Hall (2003) articulates: 'A whole historical and ideological development, then, is already presupposed in – but hidden within – the notion of the natural individual and of universal "human nature"' (Hall, 2003: 115). Marx argues in his critiques of the Hegelian dialectic in *The Critique of Hegel's Dialectic* (1992) that Hegelian 'moments' are 'moments of itself – because the moment has become for it a moment of thought, thought takes in its reality to be a self-confirmation of itself' (Hall, 2003: 121). Thus, 'the history of Man [*sic*] is transformed into the history of abstraction … the act of abstraction … revolves within its own circle' (Hall, 2003: 121). As Harvey (2018a) notes, in Marx's method the notion of abstraction becomes a tool in order to 'arrive at similar scientific forms of understanding' (Harvey, 2018a: 18). Here, scientific denotes what one might call the social sciences, in juxtaposition to say, the positivism and empiricism often attributed to the disciplines of chemistry and physics, and so on.

In *Grundrisse: Foundations of the Critique of Political Economy* (1993 [1857]), Marx argues 'production thus produces not only the object but also the manner of consumption, not only objectively but also subjectively' (Marx, 1993: 92). In this sense, production is socially situated and dynamic insofar that 'production outside society is as absurd as language without individuals living and talking together' (Marx, 1993: 84). Production like languages are thus social processes embodied as social relations between people. Marx (1993) goes on to sketch out what he calls the immediate identities between production and consumption. Marx argues that production is consumption and vice versa. This relation appears as a meditation and mutual dependence on one another yet, immediate identities here take another form. Marx goes on to argue that 'apart from being immediately the other [production and consumption], and apart from mediating the other, in addition to this creates the other in completing itself, and creates itself as the other' (Marx, 1993: 93). Stuart Hall (2003) interprets Marx's thought here, as, 'as immediate identities reign, at this simple level, identical propositions can be reversed, if A = B, then B = A' (Hall, 2003: 122). Here I would like to expand on Hall's analysis insofar that if there is consumption-inside-production and production-inside-consumption then this may have implications for how one thinks about the production and consumption of 'culture' and objects associated with culture in Interculturality. Is it that culture, with productive and consumptive relations, shall be seen as emerging from the materiality of the political economy? From a dialectical perspective then, yes. I will elaborate on this discussion further in the next chapter of the book when bringing commodities and commodity-like relations into the analytic. At this juncture, I feel the need to elaborate on my interpretation of dialectics. Dialectics does not mean that a Marxian critique of political economy does not include the dynamic production of social relations nor does it mean that the immaterial (e.g. social relationships) should be completely disregarded. This argument can be captured by Harvey's (2018a) discussion on commodities, where Marx argues that the materiality of the commodity cannot be commensurable, insofar that commodities 'cannot be a geometrical, physical, chemical or other natural property' (Marx, 1990 in Harvey, 2018a: 19). This argument is supported in Hall (2003), who argues that consumption produces production by providing 'the "ideal", "internally impelling cause", the "motive", "internal image", "drive" "purpose" for reproduction' (Hall, 2003: 123). In this sense, the Marxian method presented (which will be elaborated further in later chapters of the book) can be considered as being neither a positivist approach nor an a-historical approach but can be understood as 'with that most difficult of theoretical models, especially to the modern spirit: a historical epistemology' (Hall, 2003: 132). An epistemology that is 'determined in the first-last instance by the "present historical organization of production"' (Hall, 2003: 136) by incorporating with it a social ontology of real-life social experiences and processes (Lefebvre, 2014).

At this juncture it is important to acknowledge how Marxism and critical realism are compatible in analysing the social and discursive construction of reality (Block, 2017; O'Regan, 2021). Firstly, it is important to note that Marx's method does not mean his method is not open to criticisms. David Harvey responds to many of these criticisms in *A Companion to Marx's Capital: The Complete Edition* (2018a). However, Marx is, and remains, an important starting point for dialectical analyses. Indeed, many of Marx's manuscripts remained incomplete, therefore, interpreting and using Marx's texts as a complete whole could be regarded as a conceptual and methodological error. Despite this, the critical realist philosopher Roy Bhaskar notes that

> Marxism became fixated on the capitalist mode of production, and anything that was given to capital from outside its circuit was downplayed or ignored: the gratuitous reproduction of labour power; the way in which workers' own creative ingenuity – which is outside the bounds of their job description – sustains the labour process. (Singh et al., 2020: 238)

Bhaskar goes on to argue, 'the neglect of spiritual presuppositions of emancipation meant that Marxism couldn't really be thoroughly true to its own critique of reification' (ibid.) – surprisingly, this echoes David Harvey's interpretation (2018a) that Marx's (1990) *Capital: A Critique of Political Economy. Vol. 1* should be read as a critique of political economy rather than *of* a political economy which might come in the future. As Harvey notes '*Capital* has a great deal to say about the scientific understanding of capitalism but not much to say about how to build a communist revolution. Nor will we find much about what a communist society would look like' (Harvey, 2018a: 8). This seemingly resonates with what Stuart Hall calls the problems of the Marxian method (Hall, 2003). In critiquing Marx's position on knowledge, Hall (2003) argues that Marx's reflections on the

> 'theoretical method', to the historical object of which it produces a knowledge: a knowledge, moreover, which – he [Marx] insists – remains 'merely speculative, merely theoretical' (there is no mistaking that 'merely') so long as practice does not, dialectically, realize it, *make it true*. (Hall, 2003: 132)

In Hall's words, political economy operates through categories, which 'attempt to identify, by means of the logic of abstraction, which remains the core of a concept through history is really a type of "essentialism"' (Hall, 2003: 116). Hall seemingly is in some agreement with Louis Althusser (2005) and what has since been called Althusser's *epistemological break* with philosophical Marxism (see e.g. Balibar et al., 1994). There is an important conceptual distinction to make here, e.g. Marx's work on *Capital* (1990), which, as I have argued in line with Harvey (2018a), should be viewed as a critique of political economy and not as a political-economic blueprint. Nonetheless, Althusser's so-called epistemological break deserves our attention because it signifies a mutation of the dialectic whereby, 'the epistemological break is always the break with humanism, but subsumed under a much more general problematic: *the transformations of the structures of the dialectic*' (Balibar et al., 1994: 164). In taking this discussion further by commenting upon Louis Althusser's *For Marx* (2005 [1969]), Hall (1985) agrees with Althusser that knowledge, therefore, must be conceptualised as the production of a practice, thus 'social relations have to be "represented in speech and language" to acquire meaning. Meaning is produced as a result of ideological or theoretical work. It is not simply a result of an empiricist epistemology' (Hall, 1985: 98).

Hall goes on to explain that

> he [Althusser] places the emphasis on where ideas appear, where mental events register or are realized, as social phenomena. That is principally, of course, in language (understood in the sense of signifying practices involving the use of signs; in the semiotic domain, the domain of meaning and representation). (Hall, 1985: 99)

In this sense, knowledge, ideas and concepts have a material existence (Hall, 1985). This material existence means there are multiple, competing systems of representation – representations in the plural, not the singular (Hall, 1985). In this sense, Althusser's (2005) notion of the imaginary, which was inspired by Jacques Lacan's (1977) psychoanalytical approach, can be seen as a direct response to Marx's abstractions (Toscano, 2008; Strauss, 2006). This movement marks the shifts in language and of accentuation; what Volosinov (1973) called the multiaccentuality of the ideological sign and the class struggles found within language.

At this juncture I am not advocating or arguing for an Althusserian break as a conceptual tool for Interculturality – but Althusser's break raises an important dialectical tension, in moving 'the subject from a *constituting* function to a *constituted* position' (Balibar et al., 1994: 169). In doing so, Althusser argues that 'the subject of the unconscious, or the speaking subject, is not the subject of history' (Balibar et al., 1994: 169). For Balibar et al., (1994) this raises the problem of the knowledge effect, thus, Althusser speculates on 'the psychological or sociological personality of the "subject of knowledge"' – which makes both knowledge, and the productive forces which shape knowledge more elusive (Balibar et al., 1994: 169).

This discussion is fruitful in not only identifying the materialist construction of reality but also discussing questions of knowledge, and in bringing together conceptual discussions on the relations between structures and peoples. This discussion will be continued in the next section whereby I will continue to problematise how representations, in relation to the subject, are continually constructed by social forces and relations.

Dialectics, discourse and representation

For Bhaskar & Callinicos (2003) reality is conceived as complex, structured and multi-layered. The conceptual relationship between Marxism and critical realism (with the 'c' and the 'r' in lowercase) can be understood as being synergetic – it's plausible that there will be Marxists within critical realism and vice versa. This does not mean, however, there will be epistemological, and perhaps more importantly, ontological departures between Marxism and critical realism. Perhaps what should be heightened at this point, though, is critical realism's attack on postmodernism rather than the complex relation it holds with the many Marxisms (I intentionally mean Marxisms in the plural in order to acknowledge the many divergent approaches within Marxist theory and philosophy).

At this juncture, I argue that it is important to quote David Harvey's interpretation of Marx whereby Harvey argues that 'Marx proposes the following idea: values, being immaterial, cannot exist without a means of representation' (Harvey, 2018a: 35). In this sense, values are social relations which one cannot feel or touch, yet they objectively exist in reality (Harvey, 2018a). Therefore, our investment here lies in analysing the means in which, and by which, representations are constructed. At this juncture, it is important for me to explain to the reader that the dialectical position I adopt in addressing the Munchausen Effect in the remaining chapters of this book is inspired by dialectical Marxist theory which brings ontology and epistemology together (e.g. Harvey, 2018a; Lefebvre, 2014; Ollman, 1976). This approach differs from structuralist interpretations of Marx's works and of language and social reality (e.g. Althusser, 2005). Henri Lefebvre argues that structuralism is 'an abuse of language, and a kind of leaning towards it as mania or an intellectual tic' (Elden et al., 2023: 42). Lefebvre's argument about the abuse of language relates to the means by which under some forms of structuralism language is fetishised as an object through a narrow analytical lens (Lefebvre, 2014). Bhaskar (1989) takes the argument on Althusser and Structuralism further by arguing Althusser's approach is an 'anti-historicist conception of the social totality … [which] leaves philosophy (including his own) without any clear role, in particular; the possibilities of any demarcation criterion between science and ideology, seem ruled out' (Bhaskar, 1989: 142–143). Thus, for Bhaskar 'Althusser tends to buy theory at the expense of experience, as he buys structure at the price of praxis and the possibility of human emancipation' (Bhaskar, 1989: 143). In the chapter that follows, I will decipher the dialectic as a mode for analysing Interculturality. The version of the dialectic which I propose for Interculturality views the social totality, social relations and people as being dynamic, multifaceted and always in processes of becoming (Lefebvre, 2014). This approach brings together analysing both structures and people, and epistemology and ontology, in deciphering the materialist reproduction of everyday life (Lefebvre, 2014).

This conceptual movement towards a dialectics of Interculturality has another function in moving beyond the conceptual, philosophical and practical impasse found within some forms of postmodernism and poststructuralist approaches within the field (see the earlier chapters in this book). In identifying some of the conceptual, practical and ethical issues surrounding postmodernism, Roy Bhaskar argues:

> Someone will say to you well, you can't just talk about something that's real, because, actually, that's just talk ... is that talk real or not? The postmodernists get suck here because, if they admit that talk is real, then at least one objects real, then you've started the subject matter of ontology. (Bhaskar & Callinicos (2003: 98)

Bhaskar goes on to articulate:

> If on the other hand they say no, that's not real, then the next time Pauline says something I just turn my head the other way, because what possible point could there be in my carrying on a dialogue with something that doesn't exist? (Bhaskar & Callinicos (2003: 98)

For Bhaskar, 'whenever we speak something about the world, whenever we have a set of beliefs, embodied in that speech or those beliefs are presuppositions about the nature of the world' (Bhaskar & Callinicos (2003: 98).

What is of interest here – and perhaps the reader will see my logic in why the previous section navigated through certain Marxian ideas – is the relationship between Bhaskar's interpretation of Marx's *Capital* (1990) and how that shaped his perspective on critical realism. For example, Bhaskar's analysis of the distinctions between exchange-value and use-value not only seemingly corresponds to Harvey's (2018a) perspective but shows the transcendental aspects of Marxian concepts rather than their static rigidity. This is evidenced by what Bhaskar calls 'the mystical elements within Marx's own positive dialectic' (Bhaskar, 2008: 321) and what Harvey (2018a) calls the 'phantom-like objectivity' of value (Harvey, 2018a: 20). In this sense, the dynamics of Marx's analytic of political economy provides an analysis of how, and by what means, subject-subject, and subject-object relations are constituted (Harvey, 2018a). In *Dialectic: The Pulse of Freedom*, Bhaskar (2008) argues that this Marxian dialectic is 'materialistic and empirically grounded, is realist, and as such, it commits him [Marx] to a subject-specific ontological and a conditional relational dialectic as well' (Bhaskar, 2008: 322). Bhaskar goes on to argue that 'ontology actually includes everything – it includes contradictions and mistakes – there's nothing that's not included within ontology. Of course, now we need to differentiate within ontology the realm of the demi-real: the realm of the illusory and the oppressive' (Bhaskar & Callinicos (2003: 105). For Bhaskar, the biggest demi-real is the reproduction of the capitalist mode of production (Bhaskar & Callinicos, 2003).

What does this mean for language and representation?

The materiality of everyday life is inseparable from language. Material forces, relations and processes thus mediate how language is used and what it is used for (see Voloshinov, 1973; Bhaskar, 2016). For Bhaskar, the social sciences, historically, has been created by many splits – between positivism and hermeneutics, between object and subject, between structure and agency, between mind, body and reason – instead of reproducing these dichotomies, 'what you have to do is try and see if there's a ground that unites those antagonists' (Bhaskar & Callinicos (2003: 100). Bhaskar's (2008; 2010; 2016) critical realism, understood as a dialectical critical realism, 'covers ontological matters of socio-historical change, epistemological questions of remedying argument or reasoning, and ethical questions of human freedom' (Bhaskar, 2016: 121). These ontological matters and epistemological questions are underpinned by the Real – the social stratification of everyday life, life which is already understood through the preordination of irrealist (see previous chapter) scientific approaches (Bhaskar, 2016). In essence, what Bhaskar is saying here is that the material stratification of everyday life cannot be removed from the analytic method of the phenomena being studied – the materiality of the everyday constructs both the analytical method and phenomena. In extending his analysis of the semiotic triangle of signifier (e.g. word) – signified (e.g. concept) – referent (e.g. object), Bhaskar (2016) brings forward the consideration of a dialectical analytic 'of both material practices and language use [which] presupposes that the world is not a closed system constituted by invariant empirical irregularities … but that it is nevertheless determined at a deeper level of reality … by the world of everyday life' (Bhaskar, 2016: 34–35).

Therefore, relations between material spaces, places and objects, and how they interact with language[s] can be understood as operating through open global systems (O'Regan, 2021). In his chapter on 'Ethics and Language' Bhaskar (2016) argues that critical realism depends 'irreducibly upon the actions of others, in the *dialectical interdependence of freedom and solidarity, discourse and praxis and the dialectics of discourse and praxis*' (Bhaskar, 2016: 101). What Bhaskar is bringing us to recognise and acknowledge here is the dialectical construction of the discursive presupposition of action – relating, to how both materiality of the real produces the discursive and the extra-discursive (e.g. power relations). Bhaskar (2016), therefore, recognises Critical Discourse Analysis (CDA) (see., Fairclough, 1992; Chouliaraki & Fairclough, 1999; Wodak, 1999; Wodak & Chilton, 2005, amongst others), and the role CDA can play within a critical realist perspective. Bhaskar (2016) agrees that any use of language presupposes the semiotic triangle, constituted by the signifier, signified and referent. However, a problem associated with the function of language can be understood through the *epistemic fallacy* in linguistic form, i.e. as a *linguistic fallacy* characterised by 'the supposition that one can analyse being in terms of the language used to describe it (or in a more mediated way, used to express our knowledge of it)' (Bhaskar, 2016: 103). Bhaskar is of the view that one's language[s] cannot capture the whole of one's being, but this linguistic fallacy is often turned into an epistemic fallacy through the *refutation of the role of the material* (Bhaskar, 2016). The second inflation of the role of language relates to *refutation of the role of the material* within the embodiment of the social, within how social reality is understood (ibid.). For Bhaskar though, the discursive, and the material need to be brought together within a critical realist analytic in which language plays an important role.

Thus, 'critical realism accords the activity of hermeneutics an absolutely indispensable role … . However, critical realism will insist

of course that all such conceptualisations are fallible and subject to critique, including explanatory critique' (Bhaskar, 2016: 105).
A dialectic method therefore recognises that language and discursive processes are 'causally conditioned by extra-discursive aspects of the social reality (including power relations, the pre-existing distribution of resources, and so on)' (Bhaskar, 2016: 106). Thus, the ways in which everyday discourses are constructed, and the representations and meanings generated through discourse, are in effect produced by the Real, i.e. material conditions and contexts. Therefore, meanings and representations are not fathomed out of thin air – they are indeed socially constituted and socially produced. This does not mean that discourse, representations and meanings are static nor structural in their characteristics, on the contrary, as Harvey's interpretation of Marx's materialist dialectics, and as Bhaskar's, recognition of the role of language within critical realism shows, social relations are always dynamic and are always moving. I believe this argument is particularly pertinent for how Interculturality (and phenomena about Interculturality) is currently understood, or perhaps, misunderstood within the field. For example, interpreting concepts and notions within Interculturality (e.g. regarding people's identities) purely from the position of epistemology can only provide a theoretical snapshot of a wider discursive process. In order to analyse discursive process and how discursive processes and acts are mediated by wider societal forces, epistemology and ontology need to be brought together through a dialectical analytic.

In order to move beyond the conceptual and practical impasse of the Munchausen Effect within Interculturality, namely the phonocentrism and egocentrism of the speaking subject, it is important to bring both the discursive and extra-discursive processes together in the development of a material and dialectic analytic. To the intercultural reader who is not versed in Marxian texts or critical realist texts this might be regarded as a surprising argument, as historically within the field there is little theoretical and/or conceptual engagement with dialectics and/or materialism (perhaps the only explicit engagement can be found in Martin & Nakayama, 1999; 2013; 2015; Zotzmann, 2017). Yet, as the previous chapters in this book have shown, whether one is analysing the Philosophical Discourse of Modernity (PDM) in relation to Interculturality, the inherent phonocentrism or egocentrism of the subject within Interculturality, or the discursive construction of meanings and representations – my argument is a simple one, all of these aspects require our immediate attention in developing an analytic which brings the material into Interculturality. The reader will note that I purposely did not write 'brings the material "'back" into Interculturality' because I would argue that despite Interculturality's proximity to the political economy (e.g. in Hall, 1959, in Hofstede, 1983, and in Byram, 1997), as evidenced by the political-economic use of intercultural models by global supranational organisations (e.g. Asia Society/OECD, 2018; Council of Europe, 2018; UNESCO, 2013; World Bank, 2010), a dialectical analytic of the *Real* conditions and materialist processes that influence Interculturality has not yet taken place. Thus, the subsequent chapters of this book will continue to sketch and map the possibilities of developing a materialist dialectic for Interculturality; in doing so, I will argue why a materialist dialectic for Interculturality is important for the field.

Synopsis: Why is a dialectical approach necessary for Interculturality?

In advocating for a dialectical approach to both language, discourse and Interculturality this chapter has argued the following points (again, these points which follow should not be seen as a reductive or prescriptive way of following my logic. Rather, I acknowledge that some of the theories discussed are quite dense so the following points should be used as an aid for further critical reflections):

- An engagement with Marxian and critical realist texts have offered a two-fold effect, firstly, an engagement with these texts have served to critique the state of the Munchausen Effect within Interculturality. Secondly, in engaging with these texts, I have argued that both the production and reproduction of language and representation cannot be separated from social relations which have in turn been produced by the political economy.
- Thus, I have argued for a dialectical analytic which includes both language and discourse, but also an approach which incorporates the materiality of the everyday for a dialectic of Interculturality.
- This dialectical mode in line with Bhaskar (2016), Harvey (2018a) and Lefebvre (2014) is dynamic and open-ended. It is not rigid nor is it fixed.

- Incorporating the *real* of the everyday means moving beyond the exclusivity of the phonocentrism and egocentrism of the speaking subject within Interculturality.
- The chapter can therefore be seen as a conceptual intervention in arguing for a dialectical praxis for Interculturality – thus, shifting the field, both practically and conceptually beyond the problems of the Munchausen Effect.
- As a methodological and analytical tool, Critical Discourse Analysis (e.g. Fairclough et al., 2002), in line with Bhaskar (2016), offers a site to analyse both the discursive and the extra-discursive (e.g. power relations and material resources) in Interculturality.
- The dialectical method I argue for in this chapter should be seen alongside recent materialist interventions within the field of applied linguistics e.g. the work of David Block (2018a; 2021), Suresh Canagarajah (2020; 2021), Monica Heller (Duchêne & Heller, 2012; Heller & McElhinny, 2017) and John O'Regan (2021; 2022), amongst others.

The next chapter of the book focuses further on developing a dialectical analytic for Interculturality by focusing on the role of commodities and commodification within Interculturality. In doing so, I bring forth the notion of community into the discussion by focusing on the social relations between people, communities and commodities.

4 Interculturality and Commodification

The Fetishisation of Social Relations

Deciphering Marx's dialectical method

This chapter marks a conceptual application of the dialectical analytic proposed for Interculturality. This movement therefore involves critiquing the ways capitalist political economy mediates social relations between people and everyday contexts and situations. Before discussing commodities and commodity fetishism and what all of this means for Interculturality, I will first guide the reader through Marxian discussions on dialectics before then bringing this back to the main issues at hand for Interculturality, namely a discussion on how political economy mediates phenomena about Interculturality. In doing so I draw out examples of commodity fetishism in relation to language and culture, and I supplement this with a discussion on the notion of community as a fetishised construct.

At this point, the reader will note that the first word in this subsection is called 'deciphering' and this is a deliberate attempt to grapple with and recognise the ways in which Marxian texts (and the concepts found within Marxian texts) have often been misinterpreted and/or misunderstood. Of course, at this point I am also acknowledging the many different theoretical approaches found within perspectives on Marx – this point relates to my discussions in previous chapters whereby Harvey (2018a) remarks that it is almost impossible to read Marx without prior influences or preconceptions. The dialectical analytic I propose starts through a discussion on materialism before then going on to discuss commodities and commodification. The logic behind this is that I first want the reader to grasp the method of what

DOI: 10.4324/9781003283713-4

I am proposing here before then applying it (both conceptually and practically) to the notions of commodities and commodity fetishism.

Problematising the dialectical

In chapter 15 of *Capital Vol. 1*, 'Machinery and Large-Scale Industry', (1990) Marx elaborates on the dialectic of historical materialism in terms of how mental conceptions, i.e. knowledge is produced and reproduced in society. Harvey (2018a) articulates that the rationale of 'the real scientific method is to identify those deep elements which explain to you why certain things go on in society the way they do' (Harvey, 2018a: 202). For Marx (1990),

> technology reveals the active relation of man to nature, the direct process of the production of his life, and thereby it also lays bare the process of the social relations of his life, and of the mental conceptions that flow from those relations. (Marx, 1990: 493)

In expanding this discussion further, Harvey's (2018a: 197) diagrammatic 'moments of the materialist dialectic' incorporates the different components of the materialist dialectic which construct the wider totality. For the purposes of the discussion for Interculturality I have adapted this figure with contextual discussions on Interculturality in mind. The moments of the materialist dialectic are shown in Figure 4.1. It is also important to note that the moments of the materialist dialectic have also been discussed in depth in John O'Regan's brilliant monograph *Global English and Political Economy* (2021: 21).

In challenging perceptions and misgivings about Marx's method of historical materialism, Harvey argues that nothing in reality (e.g. knowledge, relationships, people and their senses of belonging) is produced out of the sky – the notions contained within the moments of the materialist dialectic are viewed dialectically and not causally (Harvey, 2018a). Thus, the moments of the materialist dialectic bring together social relations, mental conceptions (i.e. knowledge), technologies, nature and so on (Harvey, 2018a). These moments are not static but always in perpetual motion. Our task, therefore, is 'to understand how the mutual interactions between them work' (Harvey, 2018a: 195). In *Capital Vol. 1* (1990) Marx demonstrates in a footnote which spans two pages (Marx, 1990: 512–513) some of the problems associated with Rene Descartes' *Discourse on the Method*

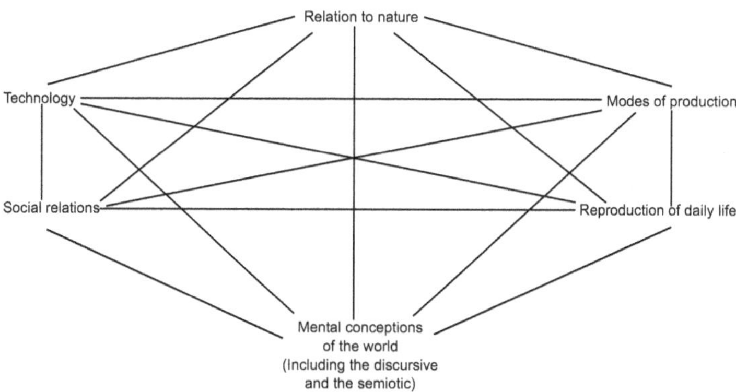

Figure 4.1 The moments of the materialist dialectic.

(2006). Marx argues that the problem with Descartes' method was that he believed 'altered methods of thought [mental conceptions in Figure 4.1] would result in an alteration in the shape of production, and the practical subjugation of nature by man' (Marx, 1990: 513). In this sense, for Descartes, attaining knowledge [mental conceptions in Figure 4.1] would be sufficient in altering the modes of production and thus the social relations produced by this shift in relations. What Marx brings us back to question, though, through the dialectic of historical materialism (shown in Figure 4.1) is that mental conceptions of, and about, the world are only one aspect of the dialectical mode of analysis and that they do not function independently from social forces. Thus,

> mental conceptions of the world can become a 'material force' in a double sense: they become 'objectified' within material objects and materialised in actual production processes. The activity of production therefore incorporates a certain knowledge of the world – knowledge that is also a social product. (Harvey, 2018b: 101)

This brings us to the point, or warning against a dialectical method focusing on methodological determinism, thus, 'no one moment prevails over the others, even as there exists within each moment the possibility of autonomous development (nature independently mutates and evolves, as do ideas, social relations, forms of daily life etc.)' (Harvey, 2018a: 198).

It is not surprising that Harvey goes on to refer to Gilles Deleuze & Felix Guattari's (1988) *A Thousand Plateaus: Capitalism and Schizophrenia* and to Henri Lefebvre's (2009) *Dialectical Materialism* in challenging the view that a dialectical method is reductive, deterministic or static in privileging one mode of the moments of the materialist dialectic (e.g. the modes of production) over another moment. For Harvey,

> all of these elements coevolve and are subject to perpetual renewal and transformation as dynamic moments within the totality … it is more like an ecological totality, what Lefebvre calls 'ensemble' or Deleuze 'assemblage', of moments coevolving within an open, dialectical manner. (Harvey, 2018a: 198)

Therefore, 'the danger for social theory is to see one of the elements as determinant of all the others' (Harvey, 2018a: 198). For example, in that 'technological determinism is as wrongheaded as environmental determinism (nature dictates)' (Harvey, 2018a: 198). In the *Grundrisse: Foundations of the Critique of Political Economy* (1993), Marx argues for a dialectical approach whereby 'mutual interaction takes place between the different moments. This the case with every organic whole' (Marx, 1993: 100). In this ecological movement Marx seems to break from what he calls the 'illusions of Hegel' which can be evidenced through the following passage:

> In this way Hegel fell into the illusion of conceiving the real as the product of thought concentrating itself, probing its own depths, and unfolding itself out of itself, by itself, whereas the method of rising from the abstract to the concrete is only the way in which thought appropriates the concrete, reproduces it as the concrete in the mind. (Marx, 1993: 101)

For Marx, this important passage, denotes a dialectical departure in thinking from Hegel's preoccupation of mental conceptions (i.e. the exclusivity attached to the moment of knowledge), towards a dialectical analytic of the *real*. It is important to note, though, that the method Marx proposes in the *Grundrisse* is applied somewhat generally in *Capital* – yet 'he [Marx] sticks to a shallow syllogistic framework given by classical political economy' (Harvey, 2018a: 369). To put this another way, one has to be aware that Marx never offers a thorough application of the method outlined in the *Grundrisse* in *Capital*. This has caused a plethora of misunderstandings and/or untoward extrapolations about Marx's writings. Harvey (2012) argues that this is complicated somewhat by the difference between Marx's scientific writings (e.g. *Capital*) and Marx's historical writings (e.g. *The Civil War in France* [1972]) which produces 'two Marxisms that are never destined to meet' (Harvey, 2012: 4). Despite, this though, the dialectical theorisation developed by Marx vital implications. Firstly, in how dialectical materialism is conceptualised (in responding to arguments that it is static or reductivist), and secondly, for Interculturality insofar that this dialectical mode can be conceptualised as an ecological totality which brings together the moments of the materialist dialectic. I mean by this? The ecological theorisation of the materialist dialectic can be seen as, and used as, a critical intervention contra to the Munchausen Effect in Interculturality.

Why is this relevant for Interculturality? If one gets besotted by linguistic determinism in Interculturality then all one will see is language, if one gets besotted with cultural determinism in Interculturality then all one will see is culture, and so on and so on. There is therefore a tendency to overlook the interrelations of things in favour of a theory or approach whereby one size fits all – in explaining and articulating everything for us. Instead, a dialectical approach for Interculturality will reveal how mental conceptions about the world (e.g. notions, concepts, values, discourses and so on) can, should be viewed, from within the ecosystem of the *real*. This *ecosystem is a relational fusion of both the material and immaterial* – this is not a relational duality; instead, it will reveal the conditions behind which mental conceptions are engendered. Therefore, the dialectical task is to understand how society functions through the moments of the dialectical totality. With regards to Interculturality one should not overlook the fact that the social relations engendered through the capitalist mode of production which has directly affected the research field in terms of how epistemic positions, bodies of knowledge, institutions and actors are constructed within society. For example, migration and emigration (i.e. the flows and movements of people) fundamentally shapes interactions between languages and cultures, and with the epistemological (knowledges) and ontological dispositions and relations within these languages, notwithstanding how one thinks about, and acts upon, their (and others) relations in the world. All these things have to some extent been produced by, or are products of, the capitalist mode of production. This means also critiquing and addressing how social injustices and inequalities are conceptualised – often, the moments of the materialist dialectic are overlooked in favour of the idealist notions of 'giving agency' and/or 'giving voice' (i.e. mental conceptions in Figure 4.1) to 'an other' (which might be a necessary and important aspect – but it might not be the *only* aspect) without acknowledging that giving agency and voice might not be necessarily addressing or redressing the *real* embodiment of material experiences and situations (e.g. immigration statuses, employment statuses and working conditions, the embodiment of social relations and power, forms of symbolic violence, notwithstanding the needs, wants and desires of the individual). I will continue this discussion in the subsequent chapter of this book on *the commons*. For now, though, the materialist dialectic discussed has provided us with a conceptual foundation, which I will now discuss in relation to commodities and commodity fetishism.

Deciphering commodities and commodity fetishism

For the interculturalist who has never read or engaged in Marxian texts this next sub-section might be a challenging read. I have intentionally tried to read Marx in his own terms to make the discussion applicable and understandable for an Intercultural audience. As I have argued throughout the book, in line with what both Harvey (2018a) and Bhaskar (2008; 2012; 2016; 2020) have written about Marx, Marx's dialectical mode goes in many directions in his analytic of the dynamic and relational modes of capitalism. Indeed, it can be even argued that Marx's dialectical mode was not finalised (e.g. see Bhaskar, 2008). Yet, in order to grapple with Marxian concepts and terminologies we need to start somewhere – and I hope the reader will find this short sub-section, both logical and necessary, for the remaining sub-sections of the chapter.

According to Marx, value is immaterial yet objective, value has a 'phantom-like objectivity' (Marx, 1990: 128) – it is 'the embodiment of human labour that has a phantom-like presence on the supermarket shelves' (Harvey, 2018a: 21). This is what Marx calls the mysterious character of the commodity form (Marx, 1990). In this sense, the experience of the commodity as a use-value has nothing to do with its value. Commodities are, therefore, 'sensuous things which are at the same time supra-sensible or social' (Harvey, 2018a: 41). Commodities can therefore be understood as definite social relations between people and things (Harvey, 2018a). Marx goes on to argue that commodities 'can have a price without having a value … [the price] in this case is imaginary … the imaginary price form may conceal a real value-relation or one derived from it' (Marx, 1990: 197). However, according to Marx (1990: 208–209), commodities have 'immanent contradiction[s]' and result in 'the conversion of things into persons and persons into things' (Harvey, 2018a: 68). This contradiction in commodities is expressed through the fetishism of the commodity. Marx defines this as 'the fetishism which attaches itself to the products of labour as soon as they are produced as commodities. This fetishism is inseparable from the production of commodities' (Marx, 1990: 161).

This means that the social processes involved in the production of commodities become objectified through labour processes. Yet, the social relations involved within these processes remain obscured by the fetishism – for example, when we go into a shop to buy something the material relations between the customer and the producer are obscured – one doesn't know, e.g., how the product was produced, how long it took or what conditions it was produced in. Marx expresses this hidden exchange through the following:

> 'To the producers, therefore, the social relations between their private labours appears as what they are' – note please especially the important phrase, *appear as what they are* – 'i.e. they do not appear as direct social relations between persons in their work, but rather as material … relations between persons and social relations between things'. (Marx, 1990: 165–166 in Harvey, 2018a: 41)

Harvey (2018a) goes on to articulate that 'we cannot abolish the fetishism, as he [Marx] earlier pointed out, we are condemned to live in a topsy-turvy world of material relations between people and social relations between things' (Harvey, 2018a: 85). What is of interest for Marx, therefore, is unpacking imaginary and fetishised relations in order to understand the contradictions produced by political economy, in this sense, the contradictions of capitalism. Marx argues 'by the virtue of being value, it [capital] has acquired the occult ability to add value to itself. It brings forth living offspring, or at least lays golden eggs' (Marx, 1990: 255). In this sense, Marx, through a materialist dialectic, is interested in what lies behind the fetishism of the commodity, i.e. why it appears to lay golden eggs (Harvey, 2018a). This fetishised ideology is what Marx (1990) calls 'accumulation for the sake of accumulation, production for the sake of production' (Marx, 1990: 742). In this sense, the ideology of capitalist accumulation means that capital must continue to expand and accumulate at all costs. Thus, the dialectical analytic presented by Marx, in critiquing the fetishism of commodities within political economy, aims to reveal the *real* conditions behind social relations, social relations which are obscured by the fetishism of things. In this sense, Marx's dialectical analytic places us in the fetish-world in order to 'understand its "illusory", "fictitious", "crazy" and "insane" character from the inside' (Harvey, 2012: 33). This argument is supported by Etienne Balibar who argues, 'fetishism is not a subjective phenomenon or a false perception of reality, as an optical illusion or a superstitious belief would be. It constitutes, rather, the way in which reality (a certain form or social structure) cannot but appear' (Balibar, 2007: 60).

So, what is Marx explicitly calling us to do? Arguably this question is provocatively addressed in the *Grundrisse* where Marx states, 'frequently the only possible answer is a critique of the question and the only solution is to negate the question' (Marx, 1993: 127). Thus, the dialectical task, therefore, is to continuously critique. This means going beyond how reality *appears* in order to ascertain the processes and relations behind which *real* conditions lie. In advancing this discussion forward, and by drawing out conceptual implications for Interculturality, I will now problematise language and culture in relation to the dialectical analytic presented in this chapter.

Language, culture and commodity fetishism

This section problematises the dialectics of language and culture as social relations whereby both language and culture shape and are shaped by materialist dialectics (Bang et al., 2007; Jack, 2004; Kramsch & Whiteside, 2008; O'Regan, 2021; Pennycook, 2021). Language and culture are inseparable dynamics that function together as a symbiotic process that embodies social relations and social realities (Kramsch 2014a; 2014b; Kramsch & Zhu, 2020). Therefore, the dialectic method presented involves bringing both the immaterial and the material together in order to make sense of the *real*. The *real* conditions which influence, constitute, produce and reproduce both language and culture. At this juncture, it is important to bring forward the fetishised belief that money is capital, as Harvey (2018a) articulates, 'the fetishism of money … conceals an underlying social reality. Money itself cannot create anything: It can only perform money functions' (Harvey, 2018a: 434). In recent times there has been a plethora of studies arguing that language, through globalisation and under conditions of late capitalism, functions as a commodity (see e.g. Heller, 2003; 2010; Holborow, 2018; Flubacher & Del Percio, 2017; Muth & Del Percio, 2018; Gray et al., 2018, amongst others). Yet, the dialectical task here means critiquing what language *appears*, i.e. what is continually metamorphosised by the dynamics of capitalism in order to reveal the *real* conditions behind which fetishised relations are engendered. For Etienne Balibar, this dialectical analytic means that commodities

> (exchange-value considered as a property of objects, the autonomous movement of commodities and prices) will have to be traced back to a real cause which has been masked and the effect of which has been inverted (as in a *camera obscura*). (Balibar, 2007: 60)

In this sense, the dialectical task for interculturalists is to *reveal* the underlying social conditions of both language and culture, whose social relations through capitalism are continually metamorphosised, and which *appear* as a transmission of light projected through a small hole in a darkened room, i.e. a *camera obscura*. Therefore, arguing whether, for example, language is commodity is not an *end* in itself – a dialectical analytic can show the *real* processes, conditions and relations which have engendered and produced the fetish-like imaginaries attached to language (and culture). This dialectical analytic runs contra to the work of Immanuel Kant which 'Marx denounce[s] as a mere variant of essentialism' (Balibar, 2007: 65) – in the sense that Kantian thought merely addresses and aims to transform mental conceptions (Figure 4.1) solely, without acknowledging the ecologic interdependency and the relations engendered between people and between people and things (Figure 4.1).

Language and the commodity

The dialectic of language is a critique of the *real* issues found within the world in which language is viewed as being a central component

(Brumfit, 1991). In their excellent article, William Simpson and John O'Regan (2018) offer a materialist critique of language by arguing that

> rather than language becoming commodified, it is more the case that language *appears* as a commodity, but is not a commodity, as the element that gives real commodities their economic *value* – expended labour, does not apply to language, because, as some scholars have pointed out, languages themselves are not products of labour. (Simpson & O'Regan, 2018: 155–156)

In echoing this argument McGill (2013) argues that the discursive metaphor of language as commodity 'is not at all the same thing as showing the actual consumption of language as a commodity' (McGill, 2013: 85). In this sense, the discursive framing of language is often equated to 'the reduction of language and languages to a commodifiable thing' (Simpson & O'Regan, 2018: 158). However, Simpson & O'Regan warn against this mode of viewing and conceptualising language insofar that

> the danger of subscribing to the commodification of everything, including language, 'all the way down', is a foreclosure on the forms of resistance to the forces of the market which exist, and which are exercised by those who work in various production processes. (Simpson & O'Regan, 2018: 161)

Therefore, language commodification cannot be viewed as a phenomenon derived from, or an effect of, late capitalism (O'Regan, 2021). As a result, academic discourses on the commodification of language (see e.g. Heller, 2010) cannot adequately argue that neoliberalism (as an emergent of political-economic forces from the 1970s onwards) can mark a temporal and historical juncture which has engendered the commodification of language (Simpson & O'Regan, 2018). To illustrate this argument, in the *Grundrisse* Marx argues that 'language does not transform ideas, so that the peculiarity of ideas is dissolved and their social character runs alongside them as a separate entity, like prices alongside commodities. Ideas do not exist separately from language' (Marx, 1993: 162–163). In fact, what Marx is alluding to here is the abstraction of value which can run through language – which, to echo previous sections of this book, is always something which is immaterial yet objective. This immateriality produces fetishised social relations between people and between people and things. In the *Grundrisse* Marx adds:

> In the development of society, not only the symbol but likewise the material corresponding to the symbol are worked out – a material from which society later tries to disentangle itself; if a symbol is not to be arbitrary, certain conditions are demanded of the material in which it is represented. The symbols for words, for example the alphabet etc., have an analogous history. Thus, the exchange value of a product creates money alongside the product. (Marx, 1993: 145)

Language thus cannot be conceptualised or understood solely from the position of discourse, i.e. mental conceptions in Figure 4.1. Treating the commodity-like *appearance* of language solely at the discursive level fails to recognise the ways in which the other components of the dialectic (Figure 4.1) are interdependent upon one another. A dialectical approach to language shifts the focus from seeing language as a commodity (as an 'end') to analysing the processes through which the materialist moments mediate social relations between language and people. Thus, applying a materialist dialectical mode to language becomes necessary in revealing the *real* relations and conditions behind which language functions (Block, 2018b). As Marx (1993 [1857]) reveals to us in his writings in the mid-19th century though, discussions on the relation between language and political economy predate academic discourses extolling the commodification of everything. Therefore, the dialectical task is to dig beneath the surface of commodification discourses in order to analyse the *real* social relations (and their contradictions). This means positing a dialectical analytic of what Marx would call '[the] material from which society later tries to disentangle itself' (Marx, 1993: 145). It is exactly this material from which society tries to disentangle where one shall turn to now.

Culture and the commodity

In previous publications I have critiqued the problematic notion of culture in Interculturality (Simpson, 2020; 2022; 2023; Simpson et al., 2022; Simpson & Dasli, 2023; Dervin & Simpson, 2021). Through postmodernism and poststructuralism culture has assumed an immaterial definition (see e.g. Dervin, 2016 who argues that both culture and the intercultural cannot be a thing because they have no agency) yet simultaneously, culture is often understood through static, rigid, and in a word – essentialist, configurations. To trace back through the theories about Intercultural Communication often one will be confronted by essentialist representations of culture often functioning as a synonym for nationality (perhaps this is best evidenced in Hofstede, 1983; Byram, 1997). This brings us to the problematique of how and why this phenomenon continues to be produced and reproduced – here I argue, we need to address the materialist dialectics through which culture functions. Culture through the moments of the political economy (Figure 4.1) becomes fetishised into being a commodity-like object. Yet, when one deconstructs the *real* social relations and conditions behind the fetishism which turns cultural artifacts and norms into cultural objects one will find contradictions which will run contra to the homogeneity presupposed in the production of the cultural object. To illustrate this argument Harvey (2002) notes the porous relation between cultural products such as the arts, food and music, and commodities such as shoes and shirts. This brings us to the question of how geography is problematised in Interculturality. David Harvey (1996) argues that often surrounding culture is a judgment and/or judgment criterion (e.g. this may include discourses about X being better than Y or that A is more distinct than B), for Harvey, such discourse

> flies in the face of historical-geographical processes of place and community construction and ignores the fact that cultures are just as relationally (and 'dialogically') constructed as individuals and a good deal more porous. Not to acknowledge these processes of cultural construction/dissolution and to build a 'particularist theory of justice' with respect to cultures as embodied *things* is to advocate a politics that would effectively freeze geographical structures of place for evermore. The effect would be as dysfunctional as it might be oppressive. (Harvey, 1996: 352)

Capitalism functions as a historical mode which simultaneously permeates and engenders the construction of both spaces and places, including both material and immaterial social relations. This inward dialectic also leads to the destruction and annihilation of space through time which can be marked as an inherent contradiction in capitalism (Harvey, 2005). However, the notion that cultures are porous and dialogical is an important argument to note. Time and time again the notion of culture in Interculturality (and generally within the intercultural) is presented as a static or fixed *thing* (which often in postmodern or poststructuralist approaches can be juxtaposed to the fluidity of identity and identities). Yet, what I find interesting here is that Harvey (1996) is warning against the embodiment of culture as a *thing* which in turn can lead to the freezing of geographical structures – in effect, the political economy of capitalism constructs knowledges, social relations and modes of being through an individual's relationality to both space and place. The production and reproduction of space and place, i.e. spatio-temporality needs to be understood through a dialectic between processes and things (Harvey, 2005). For Harvey, capitalism functions through spatial-temporal fixes which become necessary in the establishment of a form of politics constructed as 'us' versus 'them' which is often mediated through political economy. For Harvey (2005):

> Capitalism, for example, creates a relatively fixed physical and social environment to match its needs at a certain moment in history only to have to face the stressful task of overthrowing those environmental conditions (e.g., patterns of resource extraction, transport networks and city forms) at a subsequent point in order to create space for further capital accumulation. (Harvey, 2005: 248)

At this juncture, it is important to remember the previous sections in this chapter on fetishism and fetishised social relations in relation to this notion that capitalism requires relatively fixed physical and social environments. My argument here is that for culture to function as a *thing* it must *appear* as a fetishised *thing* engendered through the dynamics of capitalism – which includes how spaces and places are geographically imagined (Anderson, 1983). Geographical imagineering can include ideologies and beliefs about individual and collective belonging, legitimacy and power are constructed (Anderson, 1983). Yet one cannot detract away from, or downplay, the role capitalism plays in fetishising spaces and places. Harvey (2000) argues that 'time-space compressions engineered through the mechanics of capital accumulation have helped produce localized reactions at a variety of scales that fetishize places and spaces, even threatening to turn them into exclusionary and separatist zones of radicalized resistance and difference' (Harvey, 2000: 555).

The fetishism of spaces and places and the *fetishism of culture as a thing* must be dialectically critiqued as emerging from the moments of the materialist dialectic (Figure 4.1). To address why, time immemorial, if you ask someone on any given street, in any context, how they understand the word culture (in one of their language repertoires), time and time again the responder will often utter a static or fixed representation of how they understand 'their' culture. In another publication, I once argued that if people only want to see culture then culture is *all* people will see (Dervin & Simpson, 2021). Culture as a fetishised thing, as an *immaterial yet objective commodity relation*, must be critiqued dialectically in order to analyse its metamorphoses and constantly shifting dynamics under capitalism. In a recent interview, the anthropologist John Comaroff argues that identities have become a form of monopoly capital (World Socialist Website, 2023). For Comaroff, if an indigenous community has a product to sell, indigenous knowledge to be patented, or resources to sell – the person or persons selling the product act as a point of articulation with the capitalist mode of production. This leads to what Comaroff calls 'the revalorization of belonging, whose material and immaterial aspects become increasingly entangled and transformed' (World Socialist Website, 2023). In this sense, rather than seeing postmodern identities as being fluid in these 'late capitalist'/ 'neoliberal times' and in viewing neoliberalism as a mechanism for the liberation and/or freedom of the individual, capitalist dynamics function through appearing to commodify people through fetishised relations. This argument is perhaps best presented in *Ethnicity, Inc* (2009) whereby Comaroff and Comaroff argue that the moment ethnically defined populations perceive themselves to share interests and have legitimate claims on the world by virtue of a shared primordial essence, their identity becomes self-validating and non-negotiable (Comaroff & Comaroff, 2009). Comaroff and Comaroff (2009) argue that this reveals the worst of faux so-called political progressivism combined with the fetishised relations of capitalism. In this sense, self-validating and non-negotiable identities function as fetishised dualisms engendering the emasculation of the subject – enclosing them, an emasculation which is achieved through the commodification of social relations.

This section has problematised the key notions of language and culture in Interculturality in relation to the commodity fetishism inherent in capitalism. The next section will extend this discussion further on the social relations between people and between people and things by bringing the notion of community into the discussion.

Interculturality and the fetishism of the community

The earlier chapters of this book problematised the Munchausen Effect in Interculturality – marked by the inherent symptoms of egocentrism and phonocentrism of the speaking subject. In response, the previous sections of this chapter have sketched out a dialectical approach for Interculturality by problematising the ways in which dialectical moments function (Figure 4.1) through engendering the social relations between people and between people and things. These materialist moments are deployed as a dialectical analytic for Interculturality – bringing together, immaterialism and materialism, mental conceptualisations (including the semiotic and discursive), social relations, the capitalist mode of production, technologies, nature and the reproduction of daily life. This dialectical movement involves critiquing Interculturality (and within societies generally speaking) in analysing the materialist production of everyday life (Lefebvre, 2014). The dialectical analytic proposed is used as a method to deconstruct Interculturality – that is, a deconstruction of the fetishised *appearance* of interculturality in revealing the *real* social relations (and their contradictions) within which Interculturality functions.

This brings us to the notion of community in Interculturality. Bearing in mind how the Munchausen Effect is produced and reproduced, in recent times I felt almost apoplectic in some situations whereby someone would declare (often uncritically) that they are a member of such-and-such cultural community and/or such-and-such linguistic community (which may or may not be true). Yet seemingly they were not open to dialogues contesting or critiquing how the membership of such communities was engendered or how the social processes and relations involved function. Questioning or critiquing 'the community' felt almost like a scared writ which no one ever should do. These interactions were not philosophical or conceptual abstractions – they were and are *real*. These interactions made me want to question the *real* processes and relations behind which these discourses were revealing themselves. Could it be that the egocentrism and phonocentrism of the speaking subject function through engendering fetishised imaginaries about how, and what, the subject *thinks* it belongs to? To put this another way, does the Munchausen Effect produce fetishised imaginaries about the notion of community?

In articulating my dialectical critique of the concept of community there are two quotes from David Harvey's (2018a) *A Companion to Marx's Capital: The Complete Edition* which require one's attention. Harvey argues that '[community] is a theme that Marx explored in the *Grundrisse*, where he described that money destroyed the ancient community by becoming the community itself, the community of money' (Harvey, 2018a: 74). Harvey goes on to demonstrate that dialectically 'we may have fantasies of belonging to this or that cultural community, but in practice Marx argues, our primary community is given by the community of money – the universal circulatory system that puts breakfast on our table – whether we like it or not' (Harvey, 2018a: 74 –75).

These quotes about community show that the material cannot be divorced from the immaterial in approaching the community from a Marxian dialectic. Like I have argued in previous sections of this chapter and in other chapters of the book, knowledge/concepts/ideas (i.e. epistemologies) do not appear out of thin air, nor do they function in a vacuum. This is also the case with one's identities, subjectivities and what one may or not belong to (i.e. ontologies) – they also do not appear out of thin air, nor do they function in a vacuum. To move beyond reductionist forms of individualism one should bear in mind the phantasmic Cartesian notion of the subject declaring 'I think therefore I am' – 'to which Marx sensibly replies that you better eat dinner first' (Harvey, 2023: 228). Thus, in moving towards a dialectical mode for interculturality one must consider the relation between ontologies and epistemologies and how both are shaped by the moments of the materialist dialectic (Figure 4.1). In this sense, one needs to analyse the ways in which communities may *appear* in order to analyse the *real* relations beyond the surface appearance.

This dialectical analytic for Interculturality does not mean that individuals or people should be conceptualised through essentialist, rigid or static representations. On the contrary, Harvey (1998) argues:

> The body (like the person and the self) is an internal relation and therefore open and porous to the world … The study of the body has to be grounded in an understanding of real spatiotemporal relations between material practices, representations, imaginaries,

> institutions, social relations, and the prevailing structures of political-economic power. (Harvey, 1998: 420)

This argument fundamentally breaks with the notion that Marxian and/or dialectical approaches to identity, the self, and people ought to be rigid and/or static. Capital, like people, is constantly dynamic and porous. Yet, under capitalism fetishised imaginaries construct social relations of how people and things *appear* to be. In Marxian texts this brings one to the important interrelationship between fetishism and alienation. Marx's concept of alienation has been a source of scholarly debate inside and outside of the Marxian tradition (e.g. see the debate on alienation between [Hardt & Negri, 2018] and [Harvey, 2018c]). Is it also important to recognise Marx's own shifts in how he defined and conceptualised his theory of alienation (Zhang, 2014). Zhang (2014: 481) argues that

> Marx's use of scientific concepts of alienation in his economic and historical phenomenology was fundamentally different from his past use of the humanist alienation conception of history… In fact, these are two completely different conceptions of alienation: the labour alienation in the *1844 Manuscript* was a humanist value postulate; the idealised essence that it formed was at odds with reality. This was a contradiction between *imaginary and real.*

Whereas, in the later *Grundrisse,* which was written in 1857 and 1858, alienation can be understood as

> labour alienation was not at fault; rather, it was capitalist production that necessarily led to the dependency of man [*sic*] on external economic forces. Hired labour necessarily created a ruling power transformed out of itself: capital. This is the actual alienation of capital and labour relations that Marx describes. (Zhang, 2014: 481)

Importantly, in the *Grundrisse* Marx defines the concept of alienation as a processes whereby 'individuals are now ruled by abstractions, whereas earlier they depended upon one another. The abstraction, or idea, however, is nothing more than the theoretical expression of those material relations which are their lord and master' (Marx, 1993: 164). In this sense, individuals, and perceptions about one's individuality, are engendered through and controlled by abstractions of capital. As

(Harvey, 2018c: 140) notes, Marx recognises 'the contradictory character of the alienation that capital entails', this can be marked by the fact that when it comes to culture, community or what Marx calls *local developments of humanity* '[capital] is destructive towards all of this, and constantly revolutionizes it' (Marx, 1993: 410). In this sense, contradictoriness of capital means it is constantly metamorphosising social relations between people and between people and things. Later in the *Grundrisse* Marx goes on to show that alienation functions through capital insofar that

> the material on which it works is *alien* material; the instrument is likewise an *alien* instrument; its labour appears as a mere accessory to their substance and hence objectifies itself in things not *belonging* to it. Indeed, living labour itself appears as alien vis-a-vis living labour capacity, whose labour it is, whose own life's expression [lebensäußerung] it is, for it has been surrendered to capital in exchange for objectified labour, for the product of labour itself. (Marx, 1993: 462)

However, as Harvey (2023) argues, alienation is not confined to the labourer alone. For Marx (1993), the contradictions within bourgeoise social order (what one may call the political-economic order of liberal democracy) constructs the objectification of the social bond between people, it is within the social bond 'where alienation and fetishism collide' (Harvey, 2023: 64). In the *Grundrisse* this can be elaborated through the following extract:

> . . . but it is an insipid notion to conceive of this merely *objective bond* as a spontaneous, natural attribute inherent in individuals and inseparable from their nature (in antithesis to their conscious knowing and willing). This bond is their product. It is a historic product. It belongs to a specific phase of their development. The alien and independent character in which it presently exists vis-a-vis individuals proves only that the latter are still engaged in the creation of the conditions of their social life, and that they have not yet begun, on the basis of these conditions, to live it. (Marx, 1993: 162)

Thus, for Marx, the social relations which engender capital objectify the social relations between people and in doing so engender the means by which individuals become alienated from one another (e.g. through class relations). These conceptual discussions lay an important conceptual foundation for the remainder of this chapter and the remaining chapters of the book.

Problematising community and people

At this juncture, it is important to remember that for Marx the way in which one can conceptualise everyday realities is through that of the dialectical totality. This totality is made up of several moments which are independent, yet they co-exist within the symbiosis of society. In this sense, the totality of capitalist political economy can be viewed as an organic open-ended totality, always moving, and always in a state of becoming. The metaphor I would like the reader to think about is that of the hydrological cycle that Harvey (2017) presents to understand the totality of political economy. There are several simultaneous processes functioning within the totality of the hydrological cycle – e.g. the conversion of heat from the sun to precipitation forming in clouds – which mark the functioning of different processes within a wider whole. Now if one applies this metaphor of totality to that of social systems and of individuals – the fabric of the everyday, then one is presented by a social totality, not determined by one exclusive factor (e.g. labour), yet of a system whereby several components are constantly interacting. This view of totality does not view people or processes as static, rigid or one-dimensional entities – instead, both people and processes are viewed as being multifaceted and contradictory. Marx reminds us that our imperative is to dialectically analyse the ways social relations between people and between people and things are constantly mediated by the forces of political economy (Marx, 1990). These forces mediate relations in terms of how people relate to one another and how they understand one another. For Harvey,

> the connection between the rise of 'print capitalism', as Anderson (1983) calls it, and the transformation of linguistic diversity into 'imagined communities' of nations that ground the modern state, is one such case in point … the repository of affectivity and as inevitably chaotic and unruly, allowed those segments to be subsumed within the general capitalistic project of the rational and orderly domination and exploitation of nature. (Harvey, 1993: 16)

Harvey, in citing Anderson (1983), makes an important point here that the ways in which people relate to, or belong to, social groups and political structures such as nation states need to be considered from the wider perspective of the totality of capitalist political economy. One's being and belonging cannot be divorced from, or separated from, the processes and forces of political economy – namely relations of capital and labour. In the *Grundrisse* Marx argues that 'the individual carries his social power, as well as his bond with society, in his pocket ... in which all individuality and peculiarity are negated and extinguished' (Marx, 1993: 157). Central to Marx's argument in the *Grundrisse* are the notions of alien labour and alien capital – Alien labour whereby 'work has become a means to stay alive rather than life being an opportunity to do work' (Ollman, 1976: 151–152), and alien capital personified by the capitalist who is in a process of alienation whereby 'the object of another man's [*sic*] activity is only something to sell, something to make profit with' (Ollman, 1976: 154). Rather than being a fusion, or togetherness of commonality, the social bonds and relations between people are often fractured and estranged from each other. Marx goes on to elaborate that the

> social character of activity, as well as the social form of the product, and the share of individuals in production here appear as something alien and objective, confronting the individuals, not as their relation to one another, but as their subordination to relations which subsist independently of them and which arise out of collisions between mutually indifferent individuals. (Marx, 1993: 157)

Instead of being a form of togetherness, social relations are fetishised by the dynamics of political economy and thus appear to one another as something *other*. Marx adds

> (at least, personal ties all appear as *personal* relations); and individuals *seem* independent (this is an independence which is at bottom merely an illusion, and it is more correctly called indifference). (Marx, 1993: 163)

Therefore, the basis of what seems to connect people on the surface engenders alienation between people as '[the] vital condition for each individual – their mutual interconnection – here appears as something alien to them, autonomous, as a thing' (Marx, 1993: 157). Marx's argument is that the dynamics of political economy engender the estrangement of people through the process of reification – turning subjective relations between people into objects, where they appear as *things*. Alienation thus marks the totality of the processes of objectification for the subject.

For Marx, capital is understood as value in motion – capital mediates social relations between people and between people and things (Marx, 1990), money capital often appears as a fetishised representation of capital – something which is immaterial yet objective (Marx, 1990). The symbolic representation of money in society

> serves as such [a dead pledge of society] only because of its social (symbolic) property; and it can have a social property only because individuals have alienated their own social relationship from themselves so that it takes the form of a thing). (Marx, 1993: 160)

The expression of capital in monetary form is now expressed by the relation between capitalist and labourer, between employee and employer as 'the worker sells his labour-power in order to acquire the means of subsistence to live. To keep from dying the worker sells his [*sic*] life' (Ollman, 1976: 170). In *Capital Vol. 1* Marx argues that 'the labour process ... is purposeful activity aimed at the production of use-values. It is an appropriation of what exists in nature for the requirements of man [*sic*]' (Marx, 1990: 290). The relation between capital and labour transfigures and transfixes the relations between people and between people and nature. For Marx, the use-value of a commodity determines its usefulness – yet the value attached to a use-value is immaterial; it is determined by social relations. For Marx capital turns social relations into *things*. Alienation is where relations of production and distribution are alien to the individual thus subordinating the individual further and further. Capital thus 'confronts individuals as *an objective relation which is independent* of them' (Marx, 1993: 161). In this sense, as an example, the production of the commodity leads to a *lack* in, and of individuality for the worker – labourers alienate themselves in the relation of the exchange of labour-power for wages. Marx elaborates that this process is one 'in which the individual in one of his [*sic*] aspects objectifies himself [*sic*] in the thing, so that his possession of the thing appears at the same time as a certain development of his [*sic*] individuality' (Marx, 1993: 221–222).

The processes of alienation cannot be expressed or understood in capital-labour relations alone. Processes of alienation permeate the social fabric of everyday life and relate to all social relations (Lefebvre, 2014). Therefore alienation, and the implications of alienation upon individuals and groups need to be considered within the wider dialectical totality of society. As Ollman articulates: 'the theory of alienation is the intellectual construct in which Marx displays the devastating effects of capitalist production on human beings, on their physical and mental states and on the social processes of which they are part' (Ollman, 1976: 131). Mental dispositions and social processes produce alienation in terms of constructing relations between individuals and their social bonds, i.e. through perceptions of belonging and yearning to communities. In the *Grundrisse* Marx argues:

> Monetary greed, or mania for wealth, necessarily brings with it the decline and fall of the ancient communities [*Gemeinwesen*]. Hence it is the antithesis to them. It is itself the community [*Gemeinwesen*] and can tolerate none other standing above it. (Marx, 1993: 223)

In this sense, capital is considered as a mediator in terms of how, and the means by which, people relate to one another. Capital now becomes a key driver in terms of what people belong to and what they identify towards '*it is itself the community*' (my emphasis). Marx adds 'money thereby directly and simultaneously becomes the *real community*, since it is the general substance of survival for all' (Marx, 1993: 225) – people simply cannot live without money in exchange for the means of subsistence. Marx, in *Capital Vol. 1* (1990), writes that fetishism mediates social relations between people – simply, relations appear other to what they are. Marx articulates the antithesis or contradiction of relations between people by arguing that bourgeoise liberalism, instead of being the realisation of equality and freedom, is characterised by 'inequality and unfreedom' (Marx, 1993: 249). The accumulation of capital and the valorisation of capital, on the one hand, gives illusions (and to some extent realities) of wealth and prosperity, yet on the other hand, social inequalities continue to rise at an unprecedented level whereby debt peonage and poor working conditions are visible throughout the world (Harvey, 2017). If capital mediates relations between people and what people *appear* to belong to and/or identify towards then what do people relate to? This question is particularly pertinent in research on Interculturality whereby the

Munchausen Effect is for the self to alienate and objectify their self, usually through discursive acts of saying and/or writing, they belong to A or B or identify as X or Y. But how are perceptions about what constitutes A and B, and X and Y engendered? For Marx one must go back to the dialectical totality to see how these moments come-into-being and how they fit within the broader totality. For Marx, the *appearance* of people belonging to this or that linguistic community or this or that cultural community (which may or may not be true) needs to be dialectically analysed, Marx argues that 'in money the community [*Gemeinwesen*] is at the same time a mere abstraction, a mere external, accidental thing for the individual, and at the same time merely a means for his [*sic*] satisfaction as an isolated individual' (Marx, 1993: 226).

Etienne Balibar extends Marx's thinking further by arguing that alienation can be a means through which to conceptualise the relationship between individuals and the notion of community. For Balibar,

> alienation means the forgetting of the real origin of ideas or generalities, but it also means inversion of the 'real' relationship between individuality and community. The splitting up of the real community of individuals is followed by a projection or transposition of the social relation onto an external 'thing', a third term ... [in one case] the idol, an abstract representation [e.g., freedom] ... in the other it is a fetish, a material thing which seems to belong to the earth, to nature, while exerting an irresistible power over individuals [e.g., as a commodity/money]. (Balibar, 2007: 76)

The engenderment of community thus has a double function. On the one hand, it fetishises and turns social relations between people into *things* whilst simultaneously marking the alienation of the subject. The subject loses their subjectivity and becomes appropriated to the object of the community. Roberto Esposito argues that community can be conceptualised through 'the dialectic of lost and found, of alienation and reappropriation, of flight and return that joins all philosophies of community in a mythology of origin' (Esposito, 2009: 16). The mythology of origins which is often present in many communities (e.g. origins around indigeneity, ethnicity, race, culture, language and so on) reproduces the dialectic of the normalisation of fear, in this sense, 'the community can survive the violence that traverses it only by shifting violence onto an enemy that is able to attract it' (Esposito,

2009: 33). In this sense, in order for communities to come-into-being the community needs an *other* which functions in juxtaposition to the values and essence of the community. In the *Grundrisse* Marx takes forward the discussion on community by arguing that capital-labour relations within political economy juxtapose relations between people, they objectify the subject through the process of alienation. This process continues through the notion of alien labour, Marx argues that

> in bourgeois society, the worker e.g. stands there purely without objectivity, subjectively; but the thing which *stands opposite* him has now become the *true community* [Gemeinwesen], which he tries to make a meal of, and which makes a meal of him. (Marx, 1993: 496)

Capital transforms the relation between people and how individuals relate to one another. Relations between people are not an abstract thought process – these processes are embodied within everyday situations, scenarios and events. Thus,

> all forms … in which the community presupposes its subjects in a specific objective unity with their conditions of production, or in which a specific subjective mode of being presupposes communities themselves as conditions of production … necessarily correspond to the development of the forces of production which is only limited, and indeed limited in principle. (Marx, 1993: 496)

The presupposition that the community exists independently in isolation from human beings is completely false. It is also a false presupposition to assume that the content and identity attached to communities exists or comes-into-being independently of materialist dialectics. Capitalist political economy influences and mediates relations between people and what they *appear* to belong to. The contradictory function of fetishised social relations means that the movement of constructing and producing given communities marks the simultaneous dissolution (and alienation) of relations between people and between people and things. In the pages that follow (497–498) in the *Grundrisse* Marx highlights four areas of dissolution of community due to the reproduction of the capitalist mode of production:

> 1. *Dissolution of the relation to earth* … 2. *Dissolution of the relations in which he* [sic] *appears as proprietor of the instrument*

> … 3 … he [*sic*] has the means of consumption in his [*sic*] possession before production … 4. *Dissolution likewise at the same time of the relations in which the workers themselves* … are appropriated as such – i.e. are slaves or serfs. (Marx, 1993: 497–498)

There are two interesting points I would like to pick up here. The first point on the dissolution of the relation to earth (or what elsewhere in the *Grundrisse* Marx refers to as the metabolic relation to nature). Capital's inherent drive to annihilate space (i.e. physical, geographical, material) through time in the pursuit of accumulation produces the inherent destruction of the environment, e.g. the extraction of natural resources. Therefore, people become alienated in relation to the environment which they are so interdependent upon. The second point I would like to make at this stage relates to the dissolution of relations between workers themselves. In this sense, the capitalist mode of production alienates and appropriates workers thus turning their relations as workers into objects. Instead of conceptualising the community as something natural or spontaneous in nature, the notion of community needs to be considered from within the totality of political economy. Communities have had important historical roles and functions in the exchange of goods, services and people which needs to be considered in terms of how these processes mediate how people relate to the community. Communities can therefore have direct economic functions, but as communities are not a commodity within the circulation of capital the community can only appear as something *commodity-like*. In *Social Capital* (2005) David Halpern argues that social values and norms in various forms of community constitute 'a stock of wealth' (Halpern [2005] in Hardt & Negri, 2009: 271) which make possible the capitalist modes of production. Here, the material (e.g. modes of production) are combined with the immaterial (e.g. social values) within communities – but there is a clear distinction, *social capital is not productive capital* meaning that the immaterial has an economic function but it is 'peripheral to the productive process proper' (Hardt & Negri, 2009: 271). What cannot be denied, though, is the extent to which the production process of capital mediate the processes of how communities come-into-being. The community can no longer be conceptualised as a metaphysical entity which is separated from relations between people and between people and things (Marx, 1990). Nor can notions of community be exclusively conceptualised through the mental conceptions of knowledge alone. The next sub-section problematises what this discussion on community from a dialectical perspective means for Interculturality.

Interculturality and the dialectics of community

Conceptualising a dialectics of Interculturality means analysing the ways capital permeates within in mediating social relations between people. As Marx eloquently notes in the *Grundrisse*, though, one must remain mindful of the fact that the perpetual drive of capital is constantly to expand beyond all borders and limits (whether this be spatial borders, technological borders or borders pertaining to the construction of knowledge). This is what Marx refers to as the inherent dynamic of capital to annihilate space through time – in a sense, the drive for shorter and shorter turnover times within the production process becomes a compulsive drive beyond all possible limits (Marx, 1993). This is what Harvey calls 'the necessary geographical expansion of capitalism [which] is therefore to be interpreted as capital in search for surplus value' (Harvey, 2018b: 96). If capital is constantly in search of surplus value then this drive for surplus value is constantly modifying and mediating relations between people and their relations to the environment, society and wider social systems and structures, in a sense, the wider totality. Capitalism thus alienates people through modifying and fetishising social relations – marking the 'transformation of … activities and relations into *things* by the action of economic *fetishes*, such as money, commodities and capital' (Lefebvre, 2014: 501). However, the dialectical movement from alienation-disalienation cannot be understood as a binary relation and instead should be understood through the dynamic of 'alienation-disalienation-new alienations' (Lefebvre, 2014: 501). Lefebvre gives the example that 'being part of a collectivity can disalienate one from solitude, but this does not preclude new alienations which may come from the collectivity itself' (Lefebvre, 2014: 502). Alienation is thus infinitely complex as Lefebvre asserts – but alienation is certainly not an end in itself. For Marx, capital transforms the social fabric and social bonds between people. In the *Grundrisse* Marx argues,

> it is an insipid notion to conceive of this merely *objective bond* as a spontaneous, natural attribute inherent in individuals and inseparable from their nature (in antithesis to their conscious knowing and willing). This bond is their product. It is a historic product …

> The alien and independent character in which it presently exists vis-a-vis individuals proves only that the latter are still engaged in the creation of the conditions of their social life, and that they have not yet begun, on the basis of these conditions, to live it. (Marx, 1993: 162)

The *objective bond* between people is 'objective' in the sense that relations between people are 'objective', i.e. they exist – yet they are immaterial as social processes. When Marx refers to the 'alien and independent' character he means the conditions of social life which estranges and alienates people – as these relations are mediated by the mode of capitalist political economy. Instead of 'freeing' people the *objective bond*, i.e. a sense of 'community' further alienates and estranges people. In *The Economic and Philosophical Manuscripts* Marx argues that 'the *true* community of man [*sic*], [is] *human* nature' (Marx, 1992: 419). By this Marx means that the fetishes of the capitalist means of production metamorphosise what it means to be human – it disrupts the relationships between people and their metabolic relation to nature (Marx, 1993). People are thus communal beings insofar that they embody 'the *totality*, the ideal totality, the subjective existence of thought' (Marx, 1992: 351). For Marx the totality encompasses all the dialectical moments presented in Figure 4.1 – dynamic moments which function as symbiotic processes within society.

In expanding the dialectical mode further, for Roy Bhaskar, the dialectical 'is not a dogma, it is not a fixed or closed system of thought; it is a process in continual motion, aiming to convert ripples into waves' (Bhaskar, 2012: 166). Bhaskar argues that critical theory has been dominated by neo-Kantian thought insofar that Immanuel Kant's transcendental subject is subjected to a performative contradiction whereby the 'synthesis required to produce knowledge, the knowledge that is produced is of a world that is still described by Humean causal laws' (Bhaskar, 2016: 193). For Bhaskar, this means scientific reasoning has often been based on the presupposition of binary analytical categories and relations such as structure versus agency, and ontology versus epistemology. There are similarities in the ways an open dialectical totality is conceptualised in the works of David Harvey (2018a), Henri Lefebvre (2014), and Bertell Ollman (1976). Bhaskar builds on this work (even though there are only a few minor references to these scholars see e.g. [Bhaskar, 2015] where Lefebvre is referenced) focusing on an open systems approach that brings together both epistemology and ontology, for Bhaskar 'systems of thought are themselves part of being. Therefore, epistemology has to be included within ontology' (Bhaskar, 2012: 166). In providing concrete examples to explore the dialectical Bhaskar (2012) gives the example of the employee who works for Ford and a Bangladeshi woman who is not unionised, frightened, maybe pregnant in arguing that the Ford worker and the Bangladeshi woman both have different consciousnesses. Thus,

> you cannot bring them together by asserting the primacy of a traditional model of class over the real interests and feelings and needs of that Bangladeshi woman. You have got to do it by appealing to the commonality of their enemies and then the particularity of their own interests and differences. You have to understand universals as dialectical rather than abstract. To be specific this means that a universal is not a uniformity. (Bhaskar, 2012: 197)

In taking this analytic further, and with some resonance with the materialist moments (found within Figure 4.1 earlier in this chapter) Bhaskar (2012: 197–198) problematises four moments as an analytic for locating the particularity of the dialectical. The dialectical can thus be understood through:

1. The universal: (the capitalist mode of production or in the example discussed, the Bangladeshi women working for the capitalist firm) as something in common with all workers;
2. Specific mediations: (i.e. an exploited female worker, perhaps, casualised labour);
3. Geo-historical rhythmics: The woman is from Bangladesh a country whose physical security is threatened by climate change and global pollution;
4. Concrete singularity: In this situation the Bangladeshi woman might be bereaving a family member which may lead to the woman feeling a sense of alienation.

Thus, all these moments bring together a dynamic and multifaceted understanding of the self and of diverse subject-object relations within a wider dialectical totality (Bhaskar, 2012). In this sense, what critical realism does is attack the idea of a 'pure' or 'complete' self, critical realism attacks 'the very ground of individualism' (Singh et al., 2020: 239). Critical realism thus acknowledges the plurality of self through questioning the means and processes by which the self comes-into-being through the dialectical interplay of social processes and systems. For Bhaskar, this marks a slight shift from Marxist texts whereby 'the problem of agency within critical realism is relocated in terms of the problem of the self. What self is that actually? Marxists still think of it as the ego effect' (Singh et al., 2020: 240). However, my argument is not that there needs to be some form of binary dialectical choice between Marxism or critical realism. On the contrary, Marxism and critical realism can be complementary as Bhaskar and Callinicos (2003) and Block (2017) assert. However, operationalising a dialectical analytic for Interculturality means recognising that there can be an epistemological and ontological tension between political economy and applied linguistics. Block argues that 'scholarship in political economy is realist as regards ontology and epistemology, which puts it in conflict with the generally dominant poststructuralist approach that permeates most current research in applied linguistics' (Block, 2017: 54). The 'problem' here lies in how some forms of poststructuralism question fixed systems and structures, i.e. realities and binary oppositions which can often slide into forms of hyper-relativism. Whereas critical realism

> acknowledges that epistemology is variable and ever-changing, and that theorising is a discursively and socially constructed activity (what Bhaskar calls the 'transitive' dimension). It also posits the existence of social structures which govern social activity even if they lie beyond our ability to grasp them (what Bhaskar calls the 'intransisitive' dimension). (Block, 2017: 55)

In developing a dialectics of Interculturality, whether one is analysing culture, language, community or any other notion, one must grapple with the epistemological and ontological contours and intricacies between political economy and applied linguistics. My argument is that critical realism can be conceptually complementary to the epistemologically and ontologically open Marxism (i.e. open systems) approach of Henri Lefebvre (2014). This approach brings together Marxist theory and sociology into interdisciplinary research areas within applied linguistics and within Interculturality. Lefebvre thus offers a dialectical approach beyond the limitations of structuralism in analysing the production and reproduction everyday life including the social relations between people (Charnock, 2010). Indeed, Lefebvre (2014) dedicates a chapter within the second volume of *Critique of Everyday Life* to the theory of the semantic field where he discusses at length theories of language within the semiotics of everyday signs and representations. This discussion should be of great interest to applied linguists and interculturalists alike.

Overall, this chapter has presented a dialectical analytic for Interculturality. In echoing a quote from Marx's *Grundrisse* from earlier in the chapter it is important to reaffirm the notion that 'ideas do not exist separately from language' (Marx, 1993:163). Interculturality and knowledge about Interculturality is not produced or reproduced in a vacuum from the dialectical totality which produces society. Political economy, as an influencing system and force of mediation can no longer be dismissed. Thus, both language and Interculturality therefore need to be considered as social relations constantly mediated by social systems and structures – social systems which simultaneously mediate and engender individuals. Individuals and systems therefore coexist within wider social processes and function mutually as processes of becoming – processes of becoming which are also processes of alienation.

Synopsis: What does this mean for Interculturality?

In the preface to the French edition of *Capital Vol. 1* Marx argues 'there is no royal road to science, and only those who do not dread the fatiguing climb of its steep paths have a chance of gaining its luminous summits' (Marx, 1990: 104). Marx's argument is that the dialectical method is no easy approach that will suddenly come up with ready-made answers and solutions. If we take the dialectical metaphor that the moments within the totality of society are constantly moving, shifting, competing and contradicting one another – then the dialectical mode at our disposal is also shifting and moving. The task, however, is to constantly critique epistemologies and beliefs that are taken as a given, 'in the theoretical method, too, the subject, society, must always be kept in mind as the presupposition' (Marx, 1993:101–102). Conceptualisations of what constitutes subjects and society cannot be divorced from the workings of capitalist political economy – they are direct products of capitalist political economy.

The dialectical analytic discussed in this chapter serves as a critical intervention for Interculturality in relation to the Munchausen Effect and can be summarised through the following points:

- Reality is not a presupposition of thought – it is not merely created or engendered solely in the mind. For too long Interculturality has been conceptualised and understood as something acquired (e.g. intercultural competencies and intercultural awareness), as a set of skills and attributes (e.g. tolerance, respect, openness), or posited as a form of knowledge obtained (e.g. that there is a right or wrong way to do and think Interculturally).
- Interculturality has been conceptualised, from essentialist to non-essentialist, from positivist to post-positivist approaches, exclusively through mental conceptualisations (i.e. epistemologies) which have negated an ontological and dialectical critique of the *real* forces within Interculturality. In a sense, historically Interculturality has often fallen into an *epistemic fallacy* (see the definition in the previous chapter). The dialectical approach presented is in response to this *epistemic fallacy*.
- A sole focus on mental conceptions in, and about, Interculturality does not reveal the ways in which structures and systems shape the ways in which individuals access mental conceptions or how structures and systems shape how mental conceptions are constantly being shaped by the metamorphoses of social relations found within a wider totality.
- A dialectic for Interculturality brings together both epistemology and ontology, in how structures, systems and individuals construct materialist realities. These realties are constantly in motion and are neither fixed nor closed, they are in fact, open.

In relation to key concepts in Interculturality:

On language as commodity-like notion:

- I agree with Simpson and O'Regan in their argument that 'rather than language becoming commodified, it is more the case that language *appears* as a commodity, but is not a commodity, as the element that gives real commodities their economic *value* – expended labour, does not apply to language, because, as some scholars have pointed out, languages themselves are not products of labour' (Simpson & O'Regan, 2018: 155–156).
- A dialectical approach to language shifts the focus from seeing language as a commodity (as an 'end') to analysing the processes through which the materialist moments mediate relations between language and people.

- Thus, applying a materialist dialectical mode to language becomes necessary in revealing the *real* relations and conditions behind which language functions (Block, 2018a).

On culture as commodity-like notion:

- Culture functions as a fetishised thing, as an *immaterial yet objective commodity relation* between people and between people and things.
- For culture to function as a *thing* it must *appear* as a fetishised *thing* engendered through the dynamics of capitalism – which includes how spaces and places are geographically imagined (Anderson, 1983).
- Geographical imagineering can include ideologies and beliefs about how individual and collective belonging, legitimacy and power are constructed.

On community:

- The dynamics of political economy engenders the estrangement of people through the process of reification – turning subjective relations between people into objects, where they appear as *things*. Alienation thus marks the totality of the processes of objectification for the subject.
- Instead of 'freeing' people the *objective bond*, i.e. a sense of 'community' further alienates and estranges people.
- Capitalism thus alienates people through modifying and fetishising social relations between people.

The next chapter expands the discussion further in developing a dialectics for Interculturality by problematising the notion of the commons.

5 Interculturality and the Commons

Interculturality within the dialectics of everyday life

Before going on to discuss what is meant by the commons and what is 'common' in Interculturality it would make logical sense to remind the reader why a dialectical approach is necessary for Interculturality. Interculturality is inherently bound up within the forces, structures and logics of capitalism. Interculturality can itself be understood as a product of social relations between people and between people and things. These social relations are ultimately mediated by societal forces through exercises of power which shapes the production and reproduction of people and their relations, their subjectivities and understanding of reality, their beliefs, language, culture and so on. Central to the functioning of the 'moments' within Interculturality is the recognition that systems and structures influence individuals – to put this simply, a movement towards the dialectics of Interculturality involves analysing the means by which capitalist political economy mediates Interculturality (viewed as a totality of moments). In earlier chapters, I have discussed the rationale for why a dialectical approach is necessary to move beyond the symptoms of the Munchausen Effect in Interculturality – namely the egocentrism and phonocentrism of the subject. The Munchausen Effect in this sense can be understood as producing direct social relations from the capitalist mode of production within everyday life. At the same time, the Munchausen Effect produces fetishised byproducts of how people understand perceptions of culture, language, community and so on. These byproducts are often, but not always, immaterial – their effects may point towards

DOI: 10.4324/9781003283713-5

real material relations but the fact that they are fetishised means that they may be obscuring more systematic and/or 'deeper' relations.

At this juncture, I want to make my argument clear to the reader. Dialectically analysing Interculturality does not mean turning Interculturality into an abstraction about political economy. On the contrary, this dialectical movement means questioning and critiquing the ways political economy shapes and influences Interculturality everyday – from micro-level interactions (e.g. interactions between people on the street, in cafes, restaurants, shops and so on) to macro-level interactions (e.g. geopolitical relations between countries at national or supernational levels). Therefore, to reveal how Interculturality functions, one must reveal how capitalist political economy is produced and reproduced within everyday life. Understanding the accumulation of capital and relations pertaining to capital though means also acknowledging the contradictions inherently within capitalism and how the contradictions within capitalism can be considered to be unjust, immoral and unethical (Fraser & Jaeggi, 2018). The contradictions found within capitalism are no accident – capitalism 'changes our everyday life and the value things have for us, along with the way we relate to them, to the world and even ourselves' (Fraser & Jaeggi, 2018: 127). In using Marx's (1978) analysis of the circulation of capital in *Capital Vol. 2* the reproduction of the circuits of capital can be conceptualised through the following formula (it is important to note the distinctive circuits whereby capital can move as commodities; as money, or as a labour process):

$$M — C<^{L}_{MP} \ldots P \ldots C' — M' \text{ (etc.).}$$

In this instance 'M' denotes Money Capital, 'C' denotes the Commodity, 'L' denotes the Labour Power and 'MP' Means of Production producing the commodity. The ellipses '…' indicate the constant repetition of the circulation process, and C′ and M′ mark both the Commodity (C′) and Money (M′) with increased surplus value. In this circulation process, the money at the end is greater than the beginning – this is the same for the commodity value at the end of the process which is greater than the commodity value at the beginning (Harvey, 2018b). In this sense, 'the two phases M — C and C′ — M′ are transformations brought out through buying and selling, whereas P, the production process, involves a material transformation in the product and the embodiment of socially necessary labour' (Harvey,

2018b: 69). The circulation process that starts and ends with money capital thus embodies profit (i.e. surplus value) within its circuit. The circuits of capital are not metaphysical abstractions though, they are in fact, dynamic social relations which in turn socially reproduce material (and mediate non-material) phenomena within everyday life (Lefebvre, 2014). In this sense,

> since capital is defined as value in motion, it must necessarily pass from one state to another which means that two or more forms of capital (and labour power) must necessarily be in the same place at the same time at the moment of transition. (Harvey, 2018b: 405)

In *Capital Vol. 2* Marx elaborates the social character of the different circuits of capital through the following argument:

> Capital, as self-valorising value, does not just comprise class relations, a definite social character that depends on the existence of labour as wage-labour. It is a movement, a circulatory process through different stages, which in turn includes the three different forms of the circulatory process. (Marx, 1978: 185)

The circuits of the circulatory process here refer to the distinct yet symbiotic processes through which capital can function and move as commodities, as money, or as a labour process. As I have deciphered and depicted in previous chapters of this book. Capital, and relations through which capital functions, must be understood as social relations. These social relations are dynamic and constantly metamorphosing. These social relations mediate relationships between people and how people relate to, and interact within, socially situated realities (e.g. discourses, language, events, situations, encounters) within everyday life. The ways in which capital mediates social relations between people cannot be divorced from the dynamics of capitalist accumulation and the fact that capital must perpetually drive beyond all necessary frontiers (e.g. geographically, spatially, politically, socially, etc.). Harvey (2018b) argues:

> In a society characterised by the division of labour and exchange and by the social relationship between labour and capital, the processes of reproduction must embrace the reproduction of labour power as well as the reproduction of the social relation between capital and labour. (Harvey, 2018b: 81)

Capitalism is thus 'highly dynamic and inevitably expansionary. Powered by the accumulation for accumulation's sake and fuelled by the exploitation of labour-power, it constitutes a permanent revolutionary force which perpetually shapes the world we live in' (Harvey, 2018b: 156). In the *Grundrisse* Marx elaborates in depth on these discussions in arguing that central to capitalist accumulation is the annihilation of space through time (Marx, 1993). This point can be taken quite literally in the sense of geographical expansion through the destruction of nature, but this also includes processes of disposition, debt peonage and the commodification of cultural forms, amongst others, which mark the appropriation of capital, labour and social relations (Harvey, 2017). Capital does not just mediate social relations between people in terms of relations expressed through employee-employer relations but also through buyer-seller relations. Perhaps a rather crude example can be found in Marx's work on accumulation and reproduction on an expanded scale (Marx, 1978). In discussing the importance of consumption by the working class Marx elaborates:

> [the capitalist] as well as his press, is frequently discontented with the way in which labour-power spends its money … on this occasion he philosophizes, waxes cultural and philanthropizes … 'The working-people have not kept up in culture with the growth of invention, and they have had things showered on them which they do not know how to use, and thus make no market for.' (Every capitalist naturally wants the worker to buy his particular commodities.). (Marx, 1978: 591)

The accumulation of capital expressed as the social reproduction of the everyday involves people (i.e. as workers) functioning within the capitalist mode of production through the multifaceted process of being a labourer (i.e. through their labour power) and a consumer (i.e. through consuming commodities). However, through his dialectical method Marx reveals to us a problem insofar that whilst capital continuously searches the means for more and more surplus value 'production and consumption cannot be kept in balance under antagonistic relations of distribution' (Harvey, 2018b: 174). If an unlikely balance between production and consumption is achieved it is probably a mere coincidence – the reality is that capital's drive for more and more surplus value causes inherent crises through imbalances between rates of production and rates of consumption. Central to the continued accumulation of capital is that processes of accumulation (i.e. expressed as a totality) must involve all facets of society (Lefebvre, 2014). The constant drive for the accumulation of capital means that capital moves through different social processes whereby 'it is both preserved and increases, [it] is valorised' (Marx, 1978: 185). For capital to be constantly valorised it must go through constant revolutionary processes (e.g. in the production process), whereby 'these periodic revolutions in value thus confirm what they ostensibly refute: the independence which value acquires capital, and which is maintained and intensified through its movement' (Marx, 1978: 185).

The important point Marx is making here is that it is illusory to assume that the processes and movement of capital are determined by the acts and behaviour of individuals (capitalists) alone. In *Capital Vol. 1* Marx describes the function of capital to self-valorise (i.e. self-create) its own accumulation processes of capital. Marx describes this through the following example:

> The higher the productivity of labour, the greater is the pressure of the workers on the means of employment, the more precarious therefore becomes the pressure of their existence, namely the sale of their own labour-power for the increase of alien wealth, or in other words the self-valorisation of capital. (Marx, 1990: 798)

Capital self-valorises i.e. it self-creates value through the creation of surplus value, but as Marx reminds us in *Capital Vol. 1*, values are immaterial yet objective – values are social relations which are often expressed through the embodiment of labour-power. Value is thus 'not a fixed metric for describing an unstable world, but an unstable, uncertain and ambivalent measure that reflects the inherent contradictions of capitalism' (Harvey, 2018b: 193). To constantly self-create value, capital must constantly revolutionise itself, whereby 'the valorisation of value takes place only within this constantly renewed movement. The movement of capital is therefore limitless' (Marx, 1990: 253). The fact that capital must be a constantly revolutionising process through driving beyond all necessary frontiers means that:

> The process of accumulation profoundly modifies and overturns the previous process. It does not abolish it. It encompasses it and introduces the fundamental contradiction between the social

> character of productive labour and the private ownership of the means of production. (Lefebvre, 2014: 617)

The processes of accumulation, and therefore of social reproduction, inherently constitute inherent antagonisms. The fact that capital must keep valorising means that it (i.e. capital) as a process produces and reproduces societal ruptures and discontinuities. Lefebvre argues that through the processes of accumulation

> antagonisms can lead to breaks; contradictions do not stop society from constituting a whole (a totality) … [Accumulation can be visualised as] a process resembling a rising spiral segmented by numerous accidents encompasses the circulator process, which from then on remains a periodicity. (Lefebvre, 2014: 617)

As Marx shows, and is here confirmed by Lefebvre, capitalism causes contradictions throughout society. These contradictions are not 'an accident' and nor are they separate from the social totality one lives in. The accumulation of capital cannot be understood as a linear state passing from A to B – instead, the visualisation of the spiral is used to show how the social processes through which capital permeates are multifaceted and dynamic – in a sense, capital is continually shaping the sociality of the everyday (Lefebvre, 2014). Central to the processes of accumulation, and the valorisation of capital as a whole, is that under capitalism 'we produce as communal beings, but not for each other as communal beings' (Fraser & Jaeggi, 2018: 129). To put this simply, in the social relations between buyers and sellers, between employees and employers '"living" human beings are the producers, not only of commodities, but also of capital itself, the very force by which they are subjugated' (Fraser & Jaeggi, 2018: 133). As I have elucidated in previous chapters of this book the dialectics of Interculturality means not only analysing economic forces and processes but how capitalism shapes and mediates the social totality of everyday life (including the material and non-material). Understanding and critiquing the processes of capitalist accumulation means situating everyday social interactions within Interculturality (i.e. through the intersections of language, culture, race, ethnicity, gender, sexuality, etc.) in acknowledging that social interactions are mediated and are constantly being transformed through the dynamics of capital. The pursuit of valorisation and surplus value, and the social antagonisms produced (e.g. racism, sexism, linguism, etc.) through this pursuit, cannot be separated from the processes of capitalist accumulation. Interculturality therefore needs to embrace the ways in which all forms of life are mediated by political economy, in this sense, 'by "forms of life", I mean social formations constructed through … "ensembles" of practices, and these include economic practices as well as social and cultural ones' (Fraser & Jaeggi, 2018: 137). For Interculturality, this dialectical movement also means continually critiquing the fact that 'knowledge is an accumulative process, and so is technology. Taken together they presuppose the elaboration of a form and are part of the specific conditions of a specific process: the accumulation of capital' (Lefebvre, 2014: 621).

The reproduction of capital therefore can be understood as a *perpetuum mobile* – a constant ongoing process (Marx, 1993). Yet the constant movement of capital brings with it inherent contradictions and crises which can have a devastating effect for individuals and groups within society (Marx, 1991). This can be evidenced by 'overproduction, speculation and crises … lead[ing] to the existence of excess capital alongside a surplus population' (Marx, 1991: 350). In more recent times, look no further than the 2008–2009 global financial crisis to see the interplay of these dynamics and the increased rise in social inequalities as a result. In order to be flexible and dynamic capital needs to constantly metamorphosise, not as compartmentalised parts or units, but as a totality (Marx, 1993). Yet in this drive for constant transformation

> society as a whole tries to consolidate and to form itself into a solid totality (or tries to) … But at the same time we witness the appearance and consolidation of the individual and of private life, and of individualism as ideology. (Lefebvre, 2014: 623)

The drive for the continuous accumulation of capital ultimately produces social antagonisms and ruptures which cannot be overcome through mere ideological illusions i.e. through fetishised social relations whereby social relations *appear* as something *other* than they are. Fetishised social relations masquerade *real* social relations between people and between people and things are therefore important to the overall circuits and movement of capital. Spatially and historically, through e.g. urbanisation and migration, relations between land, capital and people have been constantly shifting and changing for hundreds, if not thousands, of years. The inherent drive for capital should be viewed as expansionary insofar that 'the production of spatial configurations can be treated as an "active moment" within the overall temporal dynamic of accumulation and social reproduction' (Harvey, 2018b: 374). These processes include phenomena such as 'colonial and neocolonial policies … the organisation of and design of space to convey social meanings … [and] class alliances built around territorial concepts such as community, region and nation' (Harvey, 2018b: 374). To put this simply, material spatial attributes need to be considered in how they contribute to the reproduction of capital through commodity production. *As capital constantly moves so do people, their identities, their languages, their beliefs and values* and so on. The movement and circulation of capital cannot be considered separate from the reproduction of everyday life – capital constructs material realities, which *is* the reproduction of everyday life. In viewing the reproduction of everyday life and the circulation of capital as an ongoing movement, an ongoing symbiosis, it means that one can also trace the social antagonisms and ruptures brought out through this dialectical interplay. Central to the reproduction of everyday life is the notion that the forces of capitalism, instead of liberating people, alienate people in dividing people from themselves (Lefebvre, 2014). One of the ways capitalism achieves this is through processes of the division of labour, David Harvey elucidates that the division of labour 'when super-imposed upon historical, religious, racial and cultural differentiations, this tendency towards geographical specialisaiton in social reproduction can take on an even more emphatic form' (Harvey, 2018b: 383).

The point Harvey is making here is that the division of labour within the capitalist mode of production reproduces societal inequalities through compartmentalising people based upon the intersections of their identity (e.g. see Bhattacharyya [2018]; Ralph & Singhal [2019]; Issar [2021]; Kundnani [2023] on the reproduction of racial capitalism and Leeb [2007]; Mandel & Shalev [2009]; Federici [2020] on the reproduction of gendered capitalism). As a result, processes through the division of labour are used to

> seize upon such differentiations and actively use them to divide and rule the working class – hence the importance of racism, sexism, nationalism, religious and ethnic prejudice to the circulation of capital. In doing so, however, capitalists support the perpetuation

> of barriers to free individual mobility, which is, in the long run, also vital to accumulation. (Harvey, 2018b: 383)

Social inequalities and injustices are important components of the reproduction of capital. For example, racism and sexism cannot be just viewed as mere by-products resulting from the capitalist mode of production – they are in fact essential to the maintenance, flow and constant reproduction of capital. Social inequalities and injustices are no accident in relation to the constant accumulation of capital, therefore, 'the mobility of capital and labour is not an unambiguous affair' (Harvey, 2018b: 385). To put this simply, the division of labour within the capitalist mode of production constitutes a form of 'social segregation [which] is based upon the division of labour, but can be reduced to it … [it] shatters, separates and dichotomizes' (Lefebvre, 2014: 624). In this sense, social divisions, social hierarchies and social inequalities need to be considered from within the totality (i.e. total movement) of capitalist political economy. Central to the continuous movement and accumulation of capital is the subjugation and appropriation of peoples and/or groups.

If Interculturality is concerned with becoming a critical praxis for addressing and redressing social inequalities – then first and foremost one needs to understand how social inequalities are continually reproduced from a dialectical perspective. This means analysing the ways capital constantly mediates social relations within society through processes of accumulation – whilst at the same time, this movement means simultaneously analysing the contradictory ruptures which serve to alienate people time immemorial. A simple step to start this process has been through analysing the ways capital metamorphoses through different circuits and how these processes shape and modify material relations between people within everyday life. A closer look into the dialectical processes of capitalist accumulation has provided the groundwork to discuss the movement of alienation-disalienation in more depth.

On alienation-disalienation

Earlier in this book I introduced the notion of epistemic fallacy to Interculturality. In dialectical thinking the epistemic fallacy is 'the analysis or definition of statements about being in terms of statements about our knowledge (of being)' (Bhaskar, 2008: 397). To put this simply, the epistemic fallacy in Interculturality is that statements about an individual's being (e.g. which may include discourses about their language and culture) are often generalised and taken as 'facts' rather than being understood as an ongoing dialectical process. In this sense, the Munchausen Effect in Interculturality can be considered a symptom of a broader epistemic fallacy. In conceptualising the Munchausen Effect as a fictitious disorder imposed onto the self then my argument here is that this movement can be undone – undone through the dialectical movement from alienation to disalienation.

For Henri Lefebvre '*the human has been formed through dehumanisation* – dialectically. The division between the human and itself was– and remains – as deep, as tragic, as necessary as the division between man and nature' (Lefebvre, 2014: 200).

There are many different forms and guises of alienation – economic (e.g. the division of labour and economic fetishes i.e. commodities, capital), social (e.g. class relations), political (relations to the State), ideological (e.g. moral doctrines) and philosophical (e.g. the separation between subjects and objects, the separation of community and individuality, the separation of truth and illusions, etc.) (Lefebvre, 2014). Within the totality of society, therefore, alienation can be understood as being 'deep and many-sided' (Lefebvre, 2014: 616). Alienation is not fixed it 'is not a 'state', anymore than disalienation is. Both are conceived of in movement' (Lefebvre, 2014: 501). Alienation and disalienation are both dynamic – they are constituted by the totality of moments within society – as my analysis has shown, these movements and processes are often mediated by the forces of political economy. Thus, rather than being an end in itself 'alienation is a result of and from something' (Marx, 1992: 429).

The dialectical movement of consciousness from alienation to disalienation is always situated and in movement. At the same time 'disalienation can be alienating and vice versa' (Lefebvre, 2014: 502). For Henri Lefebvre the point at which someone becomes aware of a form of alienation this moment automatically becomes disalienation – yet this movement can equally produce new-alienations (e.g. through feelings of hopelessness and frustration) (Lefebvre, 2014). Instead of conceptualising the movement from alienation to disalienation in a binary sense Lefebvre instead argues that this movement should be understood through the shifting dynamics of 'alienation-disalienation-new alienation' (Lefebvre, 2014: 501). For example, a woman may feel they move from alienation to disalienation through understanding the class relations and social hierarchies in their workplace. Yet, they could at the same time move from disalienation in one aspect of their life to possible new-alienations at home within their family context (e.g. in relations surrounding their domestic labour [Federici, 2018a]). The dialectic of alienation-disalienation-new alienations is not singular – it is multifaceted as the components of an individual's alienation are dynamic and constantly metamorphosing as social relations. Central to this dialectic, but not exclusively so, is the function of political economy through everyday life whereby 'money symbolizes the tearing of man from himself, it is more than the symbol of alienation, it is the alienation of man itself' (Lefebvre, 2014: 180). As I have discussed earlier in this chapter, the dynamics of capitalist accumulation serves as a reproductive force in alienating people from each other.

In the *Economic and Philosophic Manuscripts of 1844*, according to Marx (1992: 429–430) alienation can be understood through the following aspects:

1. 'man is alienated from the products of his activity, which belong to another (the capitalist);
2. man is alienated from his productive activity itself (i.e. work) … which is a negation of his essential nature;
3. man is alienated from his own essential nature, his human activity;
4. man is alienated from other men, from the community'.

Alienation, in this sense economic, social and political alienation, can be understood as an 'obstacle to freedom and a form of domination' (Fraser & Jaeggi, 2018: 134). This analysis is discussed by Rosa Luxemburg in *The Accumulation of Capital* (2003) who argues, 'the solution envisaged by Marx lies in the dialectical conflict that capitalism needs non-capitalist social organisations as the setting for its development, that it proceeds by assimilating the very conditions which alone can ensure its own existence' (Luxemburg, 2003: 346).

The operative word here used by Luxemburg is 'assimilating' in the sense that capitalism fetishises the social needs and wants required by people in order to live. However, what people need to live is not necessarily captured in the actual needs and wants of their means of subsistence – instead, capitalism whilst *appearing to* satisfy individuals' needs and wants alienates and emasculates the subject further through the processes of accumulation. Thus, 'the realisation of labour is its objectification. In the sphere of political economy this realisation of labour appears as a *loss of reality* for the worker, objectification as *loss of and bondage to the object*, and appropriation as *estrangement*, as *alienation*' (Marx, 1992: 324).

As a result, 'the worker emerges not only not richer, but emerges rather poorer than the process than he [sic] entered' (Marx, 1993: 452–453). Thus 'labour is *external* to the worker' (Marx, 1992: 326) – for example, the production of the commodity being produced is turned into something alien which does not belong to people producing the commodity. The social reproduction of alienation from within the dialectic of society can be expressed through 'power as impotence, procreation as emasculation' (Marx, 1992: 327). Power of impotence refers to the mediation of the self-alienation processes someone may feel (e.g. feelings of estrangement and loneliness in life) by capital which can further isolate and marginalise people. Whereas procreation as emasculation is taken in a literal sense to mean the increases in population required for labour power within the capitalist mode of production. In this sense, the more labour conceived for capital the more alienation to come for those (working) people. Rather, than 'liberating' and/or 'freeing' people the capitalist mode of production thus disconnects the social bond between people and becomes the driving force for the continued reproduction of social inequalities and injustices (Fraser & Jaeggi, 2018).

In Interculturality arguing for epistemological diversity (e.g. Portera, 2008; R'boul 2022a; 2022b) in separation from wider ontological struggles will merely reproduce epistemic fallacies if the production and reproduction of the dialectic of alienation-disalienation new-alienations (Lefebvre, 2014) is not addressed and redressed. This movement means critiquing the real causes of alienation in society and not merely addressing fetishised imaginaries of how things *appear* to be. This dialectical movement means bringing together both epistemology and ontology together, structures, processes and individuals in addressing and redressing the ways structural injustices are reproduced through capitalist political economy within everyday life. These issues cannot be addressed and redressed through epistemology alone. This dialectical process is socially necessary for Interculturality to be a truly critical form of praxis, but this process will not be initiated without challenges, Lefebvre argues, 'in a society that has not yet gone beyond this stage of alienation, where people have not yet regained their identity, consciousness can only be uncertain, painful and conflicted: the consciousness of the slave, the devotee or the mystified' (Elden et al., 2023: 93).

In this sense, Interculturality may have to be epistemologically broken (in recognising the historicity of the notion), in order to move to, and to facilitate, processes of disalienation. These processes may cause new-alienations as ultimately people will still be working/living/acting/interacting within a capitalist system and structure. However, if Interculturality is serious about combatting societal issues such as racism, sexism, xenophobia, etc., this movement is necessary.

On the (re)production of communal life

From the outset of this chapter, the dialectical task has been to problematise the ways capital mediates social relations between people and perceptions of their social bond. This is relevant for Interculturality insofar as conceptualising a way to understand how people socially relate to one another but also it can shed light on how relations between people can in fact divide them (e.g. through alienation). Often in Interculturality, analytical emphasis is placed upon the differences in interactions between people – whether that be cultural differences, linguistic differences or the different intersections that make people different to one another. For the remainder of this chapter, instead, I want to problematise what people have in common, as human beings, in order to discuss the possibility of whether Interculturality can be conceptualised as a form of critical and transformational praxis. This critical praxis is essential if Interculturality is to break beyond the symptoms of the Munchausen Effect. In moving towards a dialectical analytic one must first elucidate the notions of sociality and communality between people.

In extending this discussion, for Henri Lefebvre

> there is no longer a single phenomenon of public, or even private life that appears in its true form. It's no longer enough to say that everything is disguised or camouflaged, everything becomes its opposite, appearance seeks to become the whole of reality and tries to make reality nothing but appearance. (Elden et al., 2023: 93)

Lefebvre is questioning the processes by which what people think they have in common is disguised or camouflaged as a *fetish*. In this sense, there is an absence between what *appears* to constitute social bonds between people and the actual reality – this reality is often expressed as a disjuncture or rupture in the sense that what one thinks connects them to someone else can alienate them further (Lefebvre, 2014). For example, people may feel the necessity to come together and fight for a particular social cause but in doing so the sense of community constructed can act as a point of negation in totalising the identities and beliefs of individuals within social groups. In thinking about the dialectical movement of alienation-disalienation-new-alienation social groups in coming together for a socio-political cause may move from alienation to disalienation which in turn can produce new alienations if members within the group become, e.g., disillusioned or disenfranchised. Although it goes without saying, the forces that influence the disillusionment of people can be understood as the mediation of social processes and relations, social relations and processes often mediated by political economy, thus 'each person experiences the collective achievements of society as the work of an alien power' (Elden et al., 2023: 93). It is not only the achievements of society that are the work of an alien power but also the failings and failures of society too. For Marx, the question is not posited in terms of whether political economy mediates senses of becoming and belonging between people but *how* political economy mediates social bonds between people. In analysing pre-capitalist societies, Marx argues:

> It is simply wrong to place exchange at the centre of communal society as the original, constituent element. It [money] originally appears, rather, in the connection of the different communities with one another, not in the relations between the different members of a single community. (Marx, 1993: 103)

The point Marx is making here relates to classical (liberal) political economists who believed that the development of capital was some metaphysical or natural force independent from social relations between people. The argument that Marx is bringing forward here is that all historical societies, communes, and forms of social living have historically traded goods and services that have involved the movement of peoples around the world. In his analysis of pre-capitalist societies in the *Grundrisse* Marx takes the purview that human beings are ultimately social beings which have collective impulses inherently built within them. However, the social and collective elements that engender human beings are modified by the forces of capitalism and make human interactions *appear* other than they are. For Marx 'the community appears itself as the first great force of production … develop[ing] particular modes of production and particular forces of production, subjective, appearing as qualities of individuals, as well as objective [ones]' (Marx, 1993: 495).

Marx's argument here is that relations of capital turn 'organic' social relations between people into 'inorganic' relations (Marx, 1993: 495) insofar that in order to have the means of subsistence to live, people need to engage in inorganic activities (e.g. working, buying and selling goods, etc.). Therefore, the historical development of communities around the world cannot be conceived as appearing from nowhere, instead, the community developed through working subjects (i.e. people) 'which correspond[s] their specific relations amongst one another and towards nature' (Marx, 1993: 495). These social relations, mediated through the development and circulation of capital, construct how people relate to one another and to nature. As a result, communal senses of language, culture and identity are all mediated within the social totality capital operates within, thus, 'as regards the individual, it is clear e.g., that he relates even to language itself as his own only as the natural member of a human community. Language as the product of an individual is an impossibility' (Marx, 1993: 490).

For Marx, language as a product of an individual is an impossibility because language is socially produced through relations between people – it simply cannot be 'owned' by an individual. Marx calls it an *abstraction of community* to assume that the only thing people have in common can be found in language – people may have languages in common but they also have the fact that in order to survive (e.g. their means of subsistence) people have to engage in political economy through working/producing/selling – aspects that people have in common. The historical development of communities and communes therefore cannot be separated from the capitalist mode of production and the circulation of capital. Marx adds that the community appears as 'the higher proprietor or as the sole proprietor' (Marx, 1993: 472) – the unity of the community is thus founded upon the propertyless of the individual and the propertyless of the individual in relation to nature. In this sense, the community can appropriate the individual through stripping them of their property and making them work for the community – all of which is masqueraded through giving the individual a fictitious sense of belonging (Marx, 1993). This is what Lefebvre calls the processes by which individuals become 'an imaginary member of a fictitious community' (Lefebvre, 2014: 112). This line of argument is extended further by the philosopher Roberto Esposito, who argues:

> If mankind is united by the universal form that brings men together, they are irreparably separated by the material interests of which they are the content, so that their sociability is balanced and contradicted by an overpowering unsociability. For this reason the community cannot become a reality or a concept. (Esposito, 2009: 70–71)

It is the materiality of capitalist political economy that divides people – expressed through the dialectic of alienation-disalienation-new-alienations, this is the notion of 'material interests' that Esposito is alluding to. The community functions as a fetishised construct in distorting social relations between people and between people and nature whilst at the same time indebting people to the *thing* through metaphysical abstractions and perceived senses of commonality – whereby, 'servitude is understood better as the result of love and community gone bad, failed, and distorted' (Hardt & Negri, 2009: 194).

In developing this argument further, Esposito uses the Latin word *communitas* composed from the Latin words *cum* (with) and *munus* (a burden or a task) thus 'the *munus* that the *communitas* shares … is a debt, a pledge, a gift … a lack … an obligation' (Esposito, 2009: 6). Esposito goes on to argue:

> For this reason *communitas* is utterly incapable of producing effects of commonality, of association [*accomunamento]*, and of communion. It doesn't keep us warm, and it doesn't protect us; on the contrary, it exposes us to the most extreme of risks: that of losing, along with our individuality, the borders that guarantee its inviolability with respect to the other; of suddenly falling into the nothing of the thing [*niente delta cosa*]. (Esposito, 2009: 140)

In Interculturality, as I have argued elsewhere (e.g. [Simpson, 2023; Simpson & Dasli, 2023]), there has been a predetermined emphasis to analyse and conceptualise what makes people inherently different from one another (e.g. linguistically, socially, culturally, etc.). I am not disputing the fact that every person is different to one another. But the arguments presented, first through Marx, Lefebvre and then Esposito have shown that often aspects of commonality can be taken for granted, or to phrase this differently, commonality is often assumed as being present and these assumptions can fundamentally alienate people. These forms of alienation are not only between people but also between people and nature, within the wider social totality. As I have problematised, assumptions about what people have in common in terms of language and culture are mediated through everyday interactions. These interactions, expressed as social relations, are mediated by the forces and processes of capitalist accumulation. Marx shows that pre-capitalist and capitalist societies contain abstractions about how communal interests and behaviour function within the circulation and reproduction of capital. The dialectic of communal life shows that instead of being a transformational force of social change *commons* are distorted by fetishised relations – the reality is that forms of community can enclose and suffocate human beings rather than liberate them. This dialectical movement can be expressed through the transitionary phases of alienation-disalienation-new-alienation. This dialectic raises an important consideration in terms of the relationship between Interculturality, freedom and the possibility of the commons. Rahel Jaeggi argues for a critique of capitalism as a form of life, thus, 'the critique of alienation and objectification, for example, garners a quite different, much less nostalgic payoff, if we analyze these elements as a frustration of the modern promise of freedom and self-determination *as such*' (Jaeggi, 2016: 65).

What has become apparent is that if Interculturality is to be considered as a form of critical praxis then it is essential to dialectically analyse the production, reproduction and movement of alienation (and capital) within society. This means addressing and redressing the ways political economy metamorphosises social relations between people and their environment. One can no longer rest upon the assumptions found within the spoken word in terms of what people have in common. If Interculturality is to break from the egocentric symptoms of the Munchausen Effect then one needs to reconsider the dialectic of freedom in relation to Interculturality.

Freedom, Interculturality and the commons as praxis

There are different means and ways to approach the notion of the commons (e.g. Hardt, 2009; 2010; Roggero, 2010; 2011). For David

Harvey 'questions of the commons are contradictory and therefore always contested. Behind these contestations lie conflicting social interests' (Harvey, 2011: 102). Indeed, ' "politics," as Jacques Rancière has remarked, "is the sphere of activity of a common that can only ever be contentious' (Harvey, 2011: 102–103). The common should therefore be understood as a permanently evolving antagonistic space within the social totality. In *Re-enchanting the World: Feminism and the Politics of the Commons* Silvia Federici argues that

> we start with a historical perspective on the commons, keeping in mind that *history itself is a common*, even when it reveals the ways in which we have been divided, provided it is narrated through a multiplicity of voices. History is our collective memory, our extended body. (Federici, 2018b: 64)

Therefore, the commons cannot be merely considered as a localised form of pre-capitalist organisation or as a form of utopian living – instead, the commons is the collective embodiment of the totality of moments which constitutes lived experiences within the everyday (Lefebvre, 2014). The self does not function in a vacuum – people simply do not experience and embody reality in isolation. Instead, people experience social realities together as a process. Thus,

> when we speak of commons, then, we do not only speak of one particular reality or a set of small-scale experiments... We speak of large-scale social formations that at times were continent-wide, like the networks of commons that in precolonial America. (Federici, 2018b: 65)

As I have outlined in my argument – capital relations and processes of accumulation distort and modify relations between people. This includes perceptions and beliefs about what people have in common. What people experience in common is not philosophical abstraction, these processes have a devastating *real* impact on everyday life, from the construction of individual identities to macro geopolitical structures, all these phenomena characterise the 'real subsumption of not only labour processes but many aspects of daily life under the power of capital in its various forms' (Harvey, 2018d: 452). The subsumption of social relations between people to capital fetishises notions of the commons, whereby

> the 'common' which is spoken of today is really that in-common which is already wholly taken over by this kind of self-dictatorship, this kind of tyranny over oneself which is the contemporary form of that brilliant modern idea: voluntary servitude. (Tronti, 2009: 73)

The voluntary servitude Tronti discusses here is the voluntary servitude to capital relations in the sense that people voluntarily subordinate themselves to capitalism. Capitalism therefore fundamentally mediates subject-subject and subject-object relations within everyday life and what is constituted as 'common interests' for people. In the *Grundrisse* Marx describes common interests as 'the many-sidedness, and autonomous development of the exchanges between self-seeking interests' (Marx, 1993: 244–245). In this sense, common interests, common traits of belonging, and relations in common between people are expressed within the social totality. Therefore, a critique of the totality will reveal the inherent contradictions which form everyday life, and how everyday life is mediated through the subsumption of capital relations in revealing the production and reproduction of alienations and new-alienations within society. This brings one to questions of freedom and why these questions of freedom are relevant for Interculturality.

For Marx, according to the Philosopher Lea Ypi, freedom can be understood as 'freedom as self-liberation and freedom as just rule' (Ypi, 2020: 282). Ypi traces the development of Marx's thoughts on freedom, which are often implicit, back to the *Economic and Philosophic Manuscripts of 1844*, whereby Marx elaborates on his critique of Hegel's conceptualisation of the state and of society (Marx, 1992). This development of Marx's thought can be also found within the *Grundrisse* where he argues that

> out of the act of exchange itself, the individual, each one of them, is reflected in himself as its exclusive and dominant (determinant) subject. With that, then, the complete freedom of the individual is posited: voluntary transaction; no force on either side; positing of the self as means, or as serving, only as means, in order to posit the self as end in itself, as dominant and primary [*ubergreifend*]. (Marx, 1993: 244)

Central to Marx's thought, for example, is that the buyers of commodities at the market (e.g. the buying of the labour-power of the worker) must come together in the exchange of buying and selling. This is the form of freedom Marx refers to in the passage. Ypi elucidates this argument succinctly:

> So, for example, under capitalist conditions, a worker has the freedom to choose whether or not to offer his labour for sale to a capitalist. But he does not have free agency because his social position determines the options available to him and significantly constrains his ability to respond to social adversity – this is why self-liberation is a collective process rather than an individual one. (Ypi, 2020: 283)

In this sense, freedom is paradoxical. The forces claiming to give liberty and freedom to people alienate them further in subsuming the person to capital, e.g. through the conversion of their labour-power as a commodity. However, the means by which capitalism distorts perceptions of freedom is not only found in capital-labour relations, the real subsumption of labour to capital is realised and expressed as the subsumption of all aspects of society to capital (Negri, 1996). The subsumption of society to capital involves the reproduction of social fetishes and illusions about freedom, Harvey argues that

> since it is hard to protest against the universal ideals of freedom, we are easily persuaded to go along with the fiction that the good freedoms (like those of market choice) far outweigh the bad freedoms (such as the freedom of capitalists to exploit the labour of others). (Harvey, 2018a: 102)

Marx's analysis of capitalist political economy thus raises moral and ethical questions about the production and reproduction of society (Fraser & Jaeggi, 2018). In this sense, 'Marx's essential ideological objective is to pinpoint the duplicity that lies at the heart of the bourgeoise concept of freedom' (Harvey, 2018a: 102) – for example, Harvey gives the illustration of George. W. Bush's rhetoric of liberty and freedom to justify the invasion of Iraq in 2003 and the construction of the Guantanamo Bay detention facility in Cuba. Look no further than the proliferation of the Military Industrial Complex and the development of private military contractors in explaining how conflicts around the world are displacing peoples from their homes and families, and destroying nature, alongside the tragic loss of human life. A fundamental force in the proliferation of these processes lies in the mantra of capitalist accumulation for the sake of accumulation (Harvey, 1998). In other words, the accumulation of capital at all costs. Marx's critique of political economy serves as an entry point to explore the moral and ethical problematique of capital from a historical perspective. In this dialectical approach the co-presence of the ethical and the historical is important in 'generat[ing] an account of ethics in the world that identifies how ethical experience can be real and irreducible, and at the same time connected to and influenced by historical conditions' (Norrie, 2010: 18). Ethical questions in Interculturality therefore need to be connected through a materialist dialectics of political economy. This movement should inform a dialectics of Interculturality for political and social activism (Ladegaard & Phipps, 2020; Phipps, 2013; Phipps & Kay, 2014; Yohannes et al., 2023). One cannot talk about struggles for social justice and equality in Interculturality, for example whether that be about language rights in a given context, or the struggles for gender and racial equality, unless an analytic of these issues incorporates a dialectical analysis of the structures, systems and processes that have proliferated these injustices in the first instance. The subsumption of life to capital incorporates the intersectional injustices of our time – Interculturality is therefore not immune from this subsumption. Interculturality, therefore, needs to be connected through a wider praxis towards social struggles and causes. This brings us to the question not of *whether* Interculturality should be reconfigured as a critical and transformative praxis but *how* Interculturality should be reconfigured as praxis.

Interculturality as a transformative commons

In (re)thinking the possibility of Interculturality as a transformative praxis it is important to remember that the collective memory of the commons already exists (Federici, 2018b). For example, 'the cultural common,' Hardt and Negri write, 'is dynamic, involving both the product of labour and the means of future production. This common is not only the earth we share but also the languages we create, the social practices we establish' (Harvey, 2011: 103). Commons, therefore, can be understood as a '*a movement of thought* aims to use categories as tools to interpret reality and to act within and against the political economy of knowledge' (Roggero, 2010: 358). Silvia Federici takes this debate further by arguing, 'we will not construct an alternative society by nostalgic returns to social forms that have already proven unable to resist the attack of capitalist relations against them. The new commons will have to be a product of our struggle' (Federici, 2018b: 65).

Interculturality, therefore, needs to locate itself within and embody the struggles of everyday life. These struggles will be multifaceted and multidimensional – but this engagement is necessary in the development of a *truly* critical form of Interculturality. As I have shown, engaging in materialist dialectics opens Interculturality up to the historicisation of social structures and processes and their influence on individuals and groups. This process of historicisation becomes an important step in locating current struggles for social justice and equality in relation to capitalist political economy. Lea Ypi elucidates that

> revolutionary events play an educative function in addition to a politically emancipatory one; their memory matters as much as its actual occurrence in bringing humanity closer to moral progress. Its occurrence, be it future-oriented or past-oriented, reveals that the force driving human beings towards historical progress is not of a natural but of a moral, historically reflexive kind. (Ypi, 2014: 280)

Interculturality thus needs to find its moral and historically reflexive voices. The overt emphasis on traditional values, concepts and competencies (e.g. respect, tolerance, openness, etc.) found within Interculturality (e.g. that are found in different Intercultural Communicative Competence or Intercultural Competence models) have failed to create a more just and equal world. Notwithstanding the fact that the ways these models and values are imposed on peoples and groups are conceptually and practically problematic (Simpson & Dervin, 2019a; 2019b; 2020). Therefore, for transformational praxis epistemology (i.e. forms of knowledge) need to be brought together with the ontological (i.e. real) struggles found within the everyday. Bhaskar expands on this argument in bringing together the intransitive and transitive dimensions of social activity – intransitive meaning the 'dimension, in which the objects of knowledge are conceived as existing and acting independently of men [*sic*]; and a transitive dimension, in which knowledge of them is seen to be produced in the social activity of science' (Bhaskar, 1975: 101). In bringing the transitive and intrinsic alongside the intransitive one can apply a materialist dialectic that is able to analyse the ways social activity reproduces knowledge but also – this dialectic can serve to reveal the real social relations behind the reproduction of knowledge – including the systematic injustices and inequalities engendered through knowledge (Bhaskar, 2012). Bhaskar adds:

> Solidarity is not substitutionism – the educators must educate themselves, as emphasised in the concept of transformed, transformative praxis: if this is not effected within emancipatory movements, they will merely replace one set of master–slave relations with another. (Bhaskar, 2016: 181)

This argument from Bhaskar is important warning for Interculturality against the recent calls for epistemological diversity and epistemological plurality (e.g. Poulter et al., 2016; Liddicoat, 2018; Mata-Benito, 2013; Elias & Mansouri, 2020) (which in some instances can include 'good' and 'important' things to consider) insofar that they should not reconstitute new master-slave relations. In this sense, calls for epistemological plurality and epistemological diversity must be accompanied by a systemic critique of the capitalist system which engendered the unequal and unjust forms of knowledge and social relations in the first instance. Calls for epistemological diversity and plurality therefore need to be situated historically within the commons of intersectional social struggles (e.g. class struggles, gender struggles, racial struggles, sexuality struggles etc.). The philosopher Mario Tronti makes an important intervention by arguing that the commons first need to unite around values, in understanding how values are socially reproduced and reproduced, before then undoing the processes that engendered the system. He argues that 'it is important to note that this mass establishes and unifies itself not around goods as much as around values, and it is this form of mass that we must be able to define, so as to then understand how it can be undone' (Tronti, 2009: 73).

For Interculturality to become a site of critical and transformational praxis it must move beyond the symptoms of the Munchausen Effect – whereby, the Munchausen Effect is seen as a materialist abscess of knowledge and practice. This means (re)politicising Interculturality through forms of social activism in shaping new commons (Blühdorn & Deflorian, 2021). Truly, critical and transformational practices therefore need to combat the struggles of the everyday in how they are embodied through the dialectical movement of alienation-disalienation. In taking a dialectical position 'it becomes possible to understand the whole and to transform it – that is, to organise the common' (Roggero, 2010: 358). Understanding the dynamics of capital and society through the various social processes of circulation means recognising that the sites of social struggles within society are also in movement too.

Interculturality as a transformational commons means constructing 'a new common of wealth open to all' (Harvey, 2011: 107). An example of *Interculturality as a transformational commons* can find Interculturality engendering a critical praxis through spaces and places as a means of establishing a new political discourse that helps to articulate existing social struggles in recognising the power of the commons in challenging dominant power systems and structures (Lefebvre, 2014). In this sense, Interculturality as a critical and transformational praxis can activate the development of social movements and activism for wider societal change (Escárcega Zamarrón, 2009; Sorrells & Sekimoto, 2015; Ladegaard & Phipps, 2020; Ferri, 2022). In this commons freedom is conceptualised as a collective process and social activity between people (Ypi, 2020). This means addressing and redressing social inequalities and injustices in Interculturality through collective means. In Interculturality, too much historical emphasis has been placed on what makes people different from one another (which can be politically used and abused as what divides/conflicts people); yes people are different and one should acknowledge this, yet there are also aspects of our everyday lives which solidarise human beings and their interactions. Solidarising Interculturality does not mean negating the identities of individuals and groups – this movement involves tracing the ways people and their identities are mediated by the subsumption of capital within everyday life. Solidarising Interculturality is necessity amidst the backdrop of the daily destruction of nature, the destruction of people and their livelihoods through the proliferation of wars, and the destruction of the social bonds and relations between people, to name but a few. Solidarising Interculturality is thus a movement grounded within real activities and relations within everyday life and in response to the conceptual egocentric and phonocentric fetishes of the Munchausen Effect. The dialectical movement of a *transformational commons* can only be realised through a critical (re)connection with struggles found within the everyday. As I have shown through my analysis of capital relations, this movement of capital and its struggles is a constant ongoing process, a continuous and historically situated process. The task for Interculturality is to embrace this movement of critical thought and action.

Synopsis: Configuring Interculturality through commons as praxis

This chapter has extended the dialectical argument presented in this book by showing the subsumption of all forms of life to capital including the dynamics of Interculturality. In doing so, I started out with a discussion on the circulation and accumulation of capital. This was necessary in locating the specific circuits capital moves around within – whilst simultaneously showing how the movement of capital involves specific social relations between people. Central to the accumulation of capital is capital's constant movement – processes which involve the ways capital mediates relations between people through processes of alienation. Thus, the constant dialectical movement of alienation-disalienation-new-alienations is an important historical construct in revealing the subsumption of all forms of life to capital. In problematising the notion of the commons I argue for the connection between Interculturality and historicisation of social struggles (e.g. for racial equality, for gender equality, for class equality, etc.) in relation to the *perpetuum mobile* of capitalist accumulation.

I thus argue for *solidarising Interculturality* as a dialectical movement grounded within real activities and relations within everyday life and in response to the conceptual egocentric and phonocentric fetishes of the Munchausen Effect through the following ways:

- Whether one discusses more traditional modes of Intercultural Competence or whether one is calling for epistemological and diversity in Intercultural Communication one needs to prevent these notions from sliding into new-alienations – insofar, that failing to recognise the real ontological causes behind the issues of social injustice and inequality may mark the continuous reproduction of the same social issues.
- The struggles for social justice and equality therefore cannot be solved by epistemology alone. This means dialectically analysing the ways all forms of everyday life are subsumed to capital in analysing both epistemologies and ontologies together.

- Calls for epistemological plurality and epistemological diversity must be accompanied by a systemic critique of the capitalist system which engendered the unequal and unjust forms of knowledge and social relations in the first instance.
- The dynamics of capitalist accumulation fetishises and masquerades social relations between people in terms of what people think and/or feel connects their social bond to one another.
- This means the dialectical task for Interculturality involves the constant critique of alienation-disalienation-new-alienations throughout society.
- I argue that a historical and collective site to conceptualise Interculturality from involves discussing whether Interculturality can be reconfigured as commons of *transformational praxis* in historicising social struggles and the injustices engendered through capitalist political economy.
- Considering Interculturality from the position of a transformational commons is an important movement in bringing forwards questions of ethics and questions of freedom in relation to how Interculturality functions within the dynamics of the capitalist system.
- Traditionally Interculturality has been founded upon models and approaches which emphasise differences (e.g. socio-cultural, linguistic, etc.) within the individual – the dialectical approach I have presented argues for the combination of individual and/or collective differences with a collective memory in order to solidarise social relations within between people within Interculturality.
- Solidarising Interculturality is thus an important step beyond the egocentrism of the Munchausen Effect.

6 Conclusion

Reconfiguring Interculturality Within the Dialectics of the Everyday

My reflexivity of writing this book

When I first started writing this book I knew I wanted to engage with Marx's (1978; 1990; 1991; 1992; 1993) scientific writings on political economy. The reason why I wanted to engage with Marx was that I felt Interculturality, and the world we live in, is heavily influenced by the forces of political economy. Including the most micro-level mundane interactions everyday, the macro-level organisation of finance and banking, the languages we speak, and the ways our identities are engendered. Linked to this was a feeling of dissatisfaction I had been through in my own research, whereby I felt in relation to different shifts within the field (Busch, 2021), that Interculturality was sliding towards 'extreme' forms of poststructuralist relativism in relation to the subjectivities of individuals and groups, and in relation to questions of ethics and how epistemologies are constructed within the field. In a sense, my concern was about the hyper-relativity of poststructuralism whereby there is seemingly a convergence between mistaking 'criticality' with poststructuralism. I would therefore question the extent to which the 'critical turn' in Intercultural Communication is really 'critical' – poststructuralist yes, critical well, that is up for debate. I found this issue particularly problematic when in recent times there have been several calls for epistemological diversity in the field as a movement towards social justice.

Therefore, my movement away from poststructuralism led me to materialist and dialectical thinking through Marx's works on political economy and the critical realist philosophy of Roy Bhaskar (2008; 2016). The sheer depth of Marx's analysis, including the many

DOI: 10.4324/9781003283713-6

contradictions and ambiguous terms he uses, is quite remarkable. In my previous undergraduate and postgraduate training in Politics and International Relations, I briefly dipped into courses on Marxism but I felt that if I was going to argue for the development of a dialectical approach for Interculturality then, as Harvey (2018a) would say, I needed to read Marx in his own terms. I had to really make sense of Marx and how his writings on political economy had evolved over time, and I had to think about how these texts were still relevant today, notwithstanding the fact of orientating these discussions towards Interculturally relevant themes and issues. At the beginning of my journey, I reflected that I thought it would be a 'big jump' to propose a dialectical approach for Interculturality. Yet the more Marx I read the more I realised that there is a lot that Marxian dialectics can say about Interculturality.

Reflections on the dialectical method presented

Arguably, one of the best quotes from Marx on his dialectical method can be found at the beginning of the *Grundrisse*. About his dialectical method, Marx states: 'frequently the only possible answer is a critique of the question and the only solution is to negate the question' (Marx, 1993: 127). In this brilliant line, Marx expresses that the premise for the dialectical method is analysing and revealing the internal contradictions within phenomena. Critiquing the question means, i.e. critiquing how things appear and/or critiquing 'easy'/ 'ready-made' solutions to complex social processes and notions. The negation of the question means being aware of how the question was constructed in the first instance so that one does not fall into the trap of the processes that constructed the question. Interculturality must therefore be a site for the continuous critique of questions and assumptions – not in a nihilistic sense, but as a praxis that is grounded within everyday life (e.g. language, discourse, social experiences, situations and moments). Dialectically analysing Interculturality from the perspective of everyday life opens Interculturality up to address and redress societal alienations (e.g. social injustices and inequalities). This includes alienations produced and reproduced by 'common' themes and issues in Interculturality such as culture, language and community. The debates and issues around these notions cannot be divorced from the capitalist system which produced them and which continues to reproduce them.

At this juncture, it is important to recognise the differing Marxian perspectives and differing perspectives on the dialectical (see e.g. [Callinicos et al., 2021] for a comprehensive overview of Marxist and post-Marxist thought). It is important to remember in line with Lefebvre (2014) that the dialectical method is a dynamic process as the material being analysed (e.g., capitalist political economy) involves dynamic social relations that are constantly metamorphosising. This open dialectical approach involves analysing the multifaceted forms of the subsumption of life to capital that are expressed everyday. For example, on the notion of racial capitalism Arun Kundnani (2021) argues that

> notions of reserve or disposable labour are also incomplete if they neglect the racial dimensions to the production and management of surplus populations under neoliberalism. Race serves as the means by which neoliberalism organises and codes the complex, dispersed boundaries between these populations and others, between the 'exploitable' and 'unexploitable', the 'free' and 'unfree', the 'deserving' and 'undeserving'. (Kundnani, 2021: 64)

Central to the dialectic of the everyday is the ways capitalism distorts and masquerades, to put this a better way it fetishises, social relations between people – alienating them and subjugating them to capital. Therefore, as an analytic Interculturality needs to be a site that brings together intersectional struggles over class, gender, race, sexuality, language, etc., in historicising these social struggles within the everyday. Interculturality, therefore, needs to be conceptualised from within wider articulations of political struggles and their corresponding articulations within the dynamics of global political economy (Bailey, 2024).

Situating the dialectical method within Interculturality

A dialectics of Interculturality means bringing together the critique of the material (e.g. labour and nature) with the non-material (e.g. language, discourse, identities, etc.) in addressing and redressing the ways capitalist political economy mediates and influences our everyday lives. This means addressing the contradictions within capitalism that distort, alienate and reproduce social inequalities. This dialectical mode for Interculturality is incredibly flexible and dynamic – it is not fixed, just like capital that is always moving and transforming through different stages, so too are people, relationships between people, and the environment and contexts around us. This means viewing Interculturality, and the components within Interculturality (such as language, discourse and culture) as being part of a wider totality. This wider totality contains the forces and power of political economy and the intersection of many multifaceted moments (i.e. components within the totality). Thus

> we will call 'moment' *the attempt the total realisation of a possibility*. Possibility offers itself, and reveals itself. It is determined and consequently it is limited and partial. Therefore to wish to live it as totality is to exhaust it as well as to fulfil it. (Lefebvre, 2014: 642)

In this sense, within the dialectical analytic of Interculturality – moments (i.e. components of Interculturality such as language and culture and their movements) are perceived, situated and distanced. Within this dialectical mode, the moments of Interculturality are never complete – they are always in movement as processes of becoming. Yet at the same time, to coin a Marxian term, moments are objective yet immaterial – they are embodied in movement as social relations (e.g. between people and between people and things), yet they are *real* – they have real effects on and within the lives of people. Relations between people may be subjective but they are simultaneously objective – they *exist* in reality. This cannot be questioned. Focusing on the dialectical internal relations of Interculturality means that 'moments make a critique – by their actions – of everyday life, and the everyday makes a critique – by its factuality – of paroxysmal moments' (Lefebvre, 2014: 650). Look no further than the paroxysmal (sudden increase of symptoms) moments of the Munchausen Effect in how it has gripped Interculturality historically. For example, in the ways knowledge has been produced and reproduced through the Philosophical Discourse of Modernity through to the inherent egocentrism and phonocentrism of the speaking subject. Thus, these conceptual symptoms of the Munchausen Effect, in their negation of ontology, do not go far enough in addressing and redressing issues of social justice and equality. If mental conceptions, i.e. epistemologies are only being focused on in Interculturality then mental conceptions alone will not address the real structural causes and effects of injustice and inequality.

At this juncture, I want to reflect upon an implicit argument in the book which I feel needs clarifying. On reflection, there is an implicit argument in the book that interactions are face-to-face relations between people. It was not my explicit intention to focus interactions which predominantly are understood this way. Of course, a significant part of our daily interactions, and in some instances the majority of interactions, may come through online, virtual platforms/apps/websites, etc. These interactions whether online or through virtual means, often still involve people, and are thus still mediated by relations of capital. However, the time of writing this book demands that I write a little more about how interactions are conceptualised given the backdrop of technological fetishism and technological alienation (Harvey, 2017; Healy, 2020). For example, I would argue in agreement with Pasquinelli (2023) that the nexus between language and technology – especially given the so-called proliferation of Artificial Technology (AI) and 'generative forms' of Artificial Intelligence is not explicitly a 'new' phenomenon as such (Pasquinelli, 2023). Pasquinelli shows that the inner code of AI is shaped not by the imitation of biological intelligence, but by the intelligence of the division of labour and of fetishised social relations between people (Pasquinelli, 2023). To put this simply, generative forms of AI is often based upon the 'free' intellectual property (i.e. free labour) of individuals in providing outputs to train algorithms. Therefore, generative AI is not constituting a new relationship between language and technology, it is merely reproducing the fetishised knowledge of capitalist political economy (Pasquinelli, 2023). In this sense, one needs to recognise the idea that the fetishisation of technology plays a crucial role in the processes of financial accumulation and valorisation (Harvey, 2017). In this sense, online AI platforms appropriate value through labour exploitation as well as 'accumulation by dispossession' (Harvey, 2004) in the form of the systematic appropriation of knowledge and data from society at large (Rikap, 2021). To put this simply, through technological fetishism 'appropriation and exploitation are integral to the making of intangible asset[s]' (Kampmann, 2024: 61). In a recent article Kampmann (2024) argues that one needs to critically analyse the organisations behind AI firms, including

> AI developed by start-up firms formerly financed by venture capital (e.g. Microsoft and Google) and by those still privately held (e.g. OpenAI). Here the analytical lens of making intangible assets

> opens up new avenues to investigate if and how AI technologies could (and should) be 'reconfigured' towards emancipatory and democratically determined ends. (Kampmann, 2024: 61)

It is very easy to become seduced by the fetishes of technology (e.g. in the sense that technology can alleviate or eradicate 'social' problems), or the fetishes of the Munchausen Effect in Interculturality, instead the dialectical task must be on reconfiguring the internal moments and structures of technology and of Interculturality towards more socially just means. Historicising the social processes of Interculturality and connecting them to political struggles can help in moving beyond fetishised ideologies about how language, culture and people function within political economy. This means also moving beyond idealised and romanticised liberal values (e.g. respect and tolerance) which are often conceptualised as being 'ends' in themselves. For example, in *Abolition Geography: Essays Towards Liberation* Ruth Wilson Gilmore explores the notion of freedom as a place not as a mere principle (Gilmore, 2022). It is therefore important to move Interculturality beyond fetishes about knowledge, which arguably instead of giving people universal freedoms, alienates and subjugates people further and further under the powers and processes of capital (Rehmann, 2013). In this sense, Kalekin-Fishman & Langman's (2015) notion of alienation being a constant critique that never goes away is an important point – as long as capitalism exists and is present there always will be alienation. The dialectical task is therefore a *perpetuum mobile*.

The task for Interculturality: Continuing the critique of the everyday

From a dialectical perspective, Interculturality can therefore be understood as an ongoing internal critique of the everyday (Lefebvre, 2014). Interculturality is always in movement as the components that constitute Interculturality can also be understood as a perpetual movement. The dialectical can be understood as the convergence within the ensemble of components that constitute the social totality of everyday life (Gardiner, 2012).

Dialectics offers a way to connect the movements within Interculturality to real social processes and systems (and their effects) through the embodiment of everyday language, discourse and Intercultural events. This mode of analysis also offers a way to simultaneously reveal the inherent contradictions and inconsistencies found within epistemological concepts and ontological means of being and becoming in the world. Fundamentally, this movement involves a critique of the social systems and processes that shape and influence everyday interactions between people and between people and things (Elden et al., 2023). Most notably, this movement involves the dialectical critique of the influence of capital and relations mediated by capital, within everyday life (Charnock, 2010). The dialectical task for Interculturality may be endless – but that does not mean it should be futile. Systematic social injustices, abuses of power, the technological fetishisation of the everyday, the human loss and suffering due to wars notwithstanding the peoples displaced and the destruction of nature, to name but a few, are constant reminders that previous versions of Interculturality have not made the world more tolerant, respectful or just. Everyday experiences of racism, xenophobia, ethnocentrism, sexism, linguism and classism continue to be proliferated, therefore, whilst these social symptoms exist – an unrelenting need for the dialectical in Interculturality remains. Whilst the dialectical might not always give immediate solutions to social issues – dialectical analyses will be able to reveal the issues and point to the causes of the issues. Understanding the causes and influences on Interculturality is as important now as it has ever been. The dialectical task is to continue these analyses.

Synopsis: Advancing the dialectics of Language and Interculturality

In summary, the main arguments presented have been:

- Interculturality has been historically conceptualised through the notion of the speaking subject – understood as an extension of modernity, the speaking subject is founded upon the rationalisation of the self.
- Understood as a symptom of the speaking subject, the Munchausen Effect can be understood as a byproduct of the Philosophical Discourse of Modernity (PDM) and is characterised by the egocentrism and phonocentrism of the subject. In research, the PDM is understood as a product of capitalist political economy in mediating and producing forms of social science research which inherently fall into an *epistemic fallacy* – reducing reality to our

knowledge about reality (Bhaskar, 2008). The epistemic fallacy negates ontology through privileging epistemology over ontology.

- Materialist approaches to language and discourse (e.g. Pêcheux [1982]; Fairclough et al., [2002]) are important analytical tools in developing a dialectical approach for Interculturality. Materialist approaches to language and discourse offer an alternative means to view the discursive construction reality in departing from the linguistic fallacy – the epistemic fallacy in linguistic form (Bhaskar, 1989). Thus, a dialectical perspective for language and discourse is important in revealing within Interculturality how everyday interactions through discourse are mediated by the forces (and contradictions) of capitalist political economy.
- Social relations between people (subject-subject) and between people and things (subject-object) are constantly mediated by the dynamic circulation and movements of capital. Interculturality is certainly not immune to these processes – the forces of political economy are embedded within Interculturality and therefore influence how notions such as language, culture and community are perceived and understood. This means (re)conceptualising notions such as language, culture and community in relation to the wider dialectical totality (i.e. through wider social processes).
- Despite calls that the field of Interculturality has become 'critical', I have shown how Interculturality is embedded within a dialectical dynamic of alienation-disalienation-new-alienations. Therefore, calls for epistemological diversity and plurality are futile unless they are connected to historical struggles (e.g. racism, sexism, classism, linguism, etc.). If calls for epistemological diversity and plurality in Interculturality are not connected to ontological struggles then they will reproduce the epistemic fallacies (often expressed in linguistic form) of the Munchausen Effect.
- The Marxian notion of alienation has shown how Interculturality, peoples, relations between peoples, and their relationship to their environment function through a wider process – the subsumption of everyday life to capital (Lefebvre, 2014; O'Kane, 2019). In attempting to move Interculturality beyond egocentric conceptualisations I have proposed a *transformative commons as praxis* in historicising Interculturality within wider debates and struggles for political change.
- I am aware of the tensions and challenges of the dialectical approach I am arguing for Interculturality. These tensions are

perhaps best summarised by Block (2017), who discusses the realism of dialectical approaches to political economy in relation to the irrealism of applied linguistics research (which includes Interculturality). Realism demands that one goes beyond mere fetishised appearances of reality and instead, the dialectical task is to unearth the contradictions through which capitalism mediates everyday life.

- The dialectical task for Interculturality, in relation to the contents of this book, is to continue an unrelenting dialectical analysis of everyday life. The reproduction of social injustices and social inequalities means that this movement is certainly not finalised. I am sure that Marx would concur that much more dialectical work in Interculturality is needed to be done – and that is what one shall do.

Bibliography

Abdallah-Pretceille, M. (2006). Interculturalism as a paradigm for thinking about diversity. *Intercultural Education*, 17(5), 475–483.

Agamben, G. (2017). *I. HOMO SACER: Sovereign Power and Bare Life*. Stanford: Stanford university Press.

Althusser, L. (1971). *Lenin and Philosophy and Other Essays* (Trans. Brewster, B.). London: New Left Books.

Althusser, L. (2005). *For Marx*. London: Verso Books.

Althusser, L. (2014). *On the Reproduction of Capitalism: Ideology and Ideological State Apparatuses*. London: Verso.

Anderson, B. (1983). *Imagined Communities: Reflections on the Origins and Spread of Nationalism*. London: Verso.

Anderson, B. (2006). *Imagined Communities: Reflections on the Origin and Spread of Nationalism*. London: Verso.

Angermuller, J. (2018). Truth after post-truth: For a Strong Programme in Discourse Studies. *Palgrave Communications*, 4(1), 1–8.

Angermuller, J., Maingueneau, D., & Wodak, R. (Eds.). (2014). *The Discourse Studies Reader: Main Currents in Theory and Analysis*. Amsterdam: John Benjamins Publishing Company.

Archer, M. (1995). *Realist Social Theory: The Morphogentic Approach*. Cambridge: Cambridge University Press.

Archer, M. (2000). *Being Human: The Problem of Agency*. Cambridge: Cambridge University Press.

Archer, M. (2010). Morphogenesis versus structuration: On combining structure and action. *British Journal of Sociology*, 61, 225–252.

Asia Society/OECD. (2018). *Teaching for Global Competence in a Rapidly Changing World*. New York: OECD Publishing https://doi.org/10.1787/9789264289024-en

Bailey, D. (2024). Weak progressive politics and resistance without guarantees in the post-pandemic global political economy: A broadly Marxist account. *Global Political Economy*, 3(1), 16–39. Retrieved April 29, 2024, from https://doi.org/10.1332/26352257Y2024D000000015

Bakhtin, M. M. (1981). *The Dialogic Imagination: Four Essays*. Austin: University of Texas Press.

Bakhtin, M. M. (2012). *Sobranie sochinenij. (T.3). Teoriia romana (1930–1961 gg.)* (Eds. Sergey Georgievich Bocharov and Vadim Valer'janovich Kozhinov). Moskva: Jazyki slavianskikh kul'tur.

Balibar, É. (1990). The nation form: History and ideology. *Review (Fernand Braudel Center)*, 13(3), 329–361.

Balibar, É. (2007). *The Philosophy of Marx*. London: Verso.

Balibar, É., & Broder, D. (2022). Reproductions. *Rethinking Marxism*, 34(2), 142–161.

Balibar, E., Cohen, M., & Robbins, B. (1994). Althusser's object. *Social Text*, 39, 157–188.

Bang, J. C., Døør, J., Nash, J., & Steffensen, S. V. (2007). *Language, Ecology and Society: A Dialectical Approach*. London: Continuum International Publishing Group.

Bauman, Z. (1997). *Postmodernity and Its Discontents*. London: John Wiley & Sons.

Bauman, Z. (2001). *Community: Seeking Safety in an Insecure World*. London: Polity.

Bhaskar, R. (1975). Forms of realism. *Philosophica*, 15(1), 99–127.

Bhaskar, R. (1989). *Reclaiming Reality: A Critical Introduction to Contemporary Philosophy*. London: Verso Books.

Bhaskar, R. (2002). *Reflections on Meta-Reality: Transcendence, Emancipation and Everyday Life*. New Delhi and London: Thousand Oaks and Sage.

Bhaskar, R. (2008). *Dialectic: The Pulse of Freedom*. London: Routledge.

Bhaskar, R. (2010). *Plato etc: Problems of Philosophy and Their Resolution*. London: Routledge.

Bhaskar, R. (2012). *From Science to Emancipation: Alienation and the Actuality of Enlightenment*. London: Routledge.

Bhaskar, R. (2015). *The Possibility of Naturalism: A Philosophical Critique of the Contemporary Human Sciences*. London: Routledge.

Bhaskar, R. (2016). *Enlightened Common Sense: The Philosophy of Critical Realism*. London: Routledge.

Bhaskar, R. (2020). Critical realism and the ontology of persons. *Journal of Critical Realism*, 19(2), 113–120.

Bhaskar, R., & Callinicos, A. (2003). Marxism and critical realism: A debate. *Journal of Critical Realism*, 1(2), 89–114.

Bhattacharyya, G. (2018). *Rethinking Racial Capitalism: Questions of Reproduction and Survival*. London: Rowman & Littlefield.

Block, D. (2013). The structure and agency dilemma in identity and intercultural communication research. *Language and Intercultural Communication*, 13(2), 126–147.

Block, D. (2014). *Social Class in Applied Linguistics*. London: Routledge.

Block, D. (2017). Political economy in applied linguistics research. *Language Teaching*, 50(1), 32–64.

Block, D. (2018a). *Political Economy and Sociolinguistics: Neoliberalism, Inequality and Social Class*. London: Bloomsbury Publishing.

Block, D. (2018b). What on earth is 'language commodification'? In Schmenk, B., Breidbach, S., & Küster, L. (Eds.), *Sloganization in Language Education Discourse: Conceptual Thinking in the Age of Academic Marketization* (121–141). Bristol, Blue Ridge Summit: Multilingual Matters. https://doi.org/10.21832/9781788921879-008

Block, D. (2021). *Innovations and Challenges in Identity Research*. London: Routledge.

Blommaert, J. (2010). *The Sociolinguistics of Globalization*. Cambridge: Cambridge University Press.

Blühdorn, I., & Deflorian, M. (2021). Politicisation beyond post-politics: New social activism and the reconfiguration of political discourse. *Social Movement Studies*, 20(3), 259–275.

Bourdieu, P. (2003). *Fighting Back: Against Tyranny of the Market 2*. London: Verso.

Bourdieu, P. (2004). *Science of Science and Reflexivity*. Cambridge: Polity.

Brandist, C. (2002). *The Bakhtin Circle: Philosophy, Culture and Politics*. London: Pluto Press.

Britzman, D. P. (2012). *Practice Makes Practice: A Critical Study of Learning to Teach*. New York: Suny Press.

Brumfit, C. (1991). Applied linguistics in higher education: Riding the storm. *BAAL Newsletter*, 38, 45–49.

Busch, D. (2021). The changing discourse of intercultural ethics: A diachronic meta-analysis. *Journal of Multicultural Discourses*, 16(3), 189–202.

Byram, M. (1997). *Teaching and Assessing Intercultural Communicative Competence*. Bristol: Multilingual Matters.

Byram, M. (2000). Assessing intercultural competence in language teaching. *Sprogforum*, 18(6), 8–13.

Byram, M. (2008). *From Foreign Language Education to Education for Intercultural Citizenship: Essays and Reflections*. Clevedon: Multilingual Matters.

Byram, M. (2021). *Teaching and Assessing Intercultural Communicative Competence* (2nd Edition). Bristol: Multilingual Matters.

Callinicos, A., Kouvélakis, E., & Pradella, L. (Eds.). (2021). *Routledge Handbook of Marxism and Post-Marxism*. London: Routledge.

Canagarajah, S. (2020). Reconsidering material conditions in language politics: A revised agenda for resistance. *Nordic Journal of English Studies*, 19(3), 101–114.

Canagarajah, S. (2021). Materialising semiotic repertoires: Challenges in the interactional analysis of multilingual communication. *International Journal of Multilingualism*, 18(2), 206–225.

Charnock, G. (2010). Challenging new state spatialities: The open Marxism of Henri Lefebvre. *Antipode*, 42(5), 1279–1303.

Chouliaraki, L., & Fairclough, N. (1999). *Discourse in Late Modernity: Rethinking Critical Discourse Analysis*. Edinburgh: Edinburgh University Press.

Comaroff, J. L., & Comaroff, J. (2009). *Ethnicity, Inc*. Chicago: University of Chicago Press.

Cooren, F., & Sandler, S. (2014). Polyphony, ventriloquism, and constitution: In dialogue with Bakhtin. *Communication Theory*, 24(3), 225–244.

Council of Europe. (2018). *Reference Framework for Democratic Culture: Volume 1: Contexts, Concepts and Model*. Strasbourg: Council of Europe Publishing.

Dasli, M., & Diaz, A. R. (Eds.). (2017). *The Critical Turn in Language and Intercultural Communication Pedagogy: Theory, Research and Practice*. London: Routledge.

Dasli, M., & Simpson, A. (2023). Introducing intercultural communication pedagogy and the question of the other. *Pedagogy, Culture & Society*, 31(2), 221–235. DOI: 10.1080/14681366.2022.2164339

Deardorff, D. K. (2019). *Manual for Developing Intercultural Competencies: Story Circles*. London: Routledge.

Deleuze, G., & Guattari, F. (1988). *A Thousand Plateaus: Capitalism and Schizophrenia*. London: Bloomsbury Publishing.

Derrida, J. (1997). *Of Grammatology*. Baltimore: John Hopkins University Press.

Dervin, F. (2011). A plea for change in research on intercultural discourses: A 'liquid' approach to the study of the acculturation of Chinese students. *Journal of Multicultural Discourses*, 6(1), 37–52.

Dervin, F. (2016). *Interculturality in Education: A Theoretical and Methodological Toolbox*. London: Palgrave Macmillan.

Dervin, F. (2017). *Critical Interculturality: Lectures and Notes*. Cambridge: Cambridge Scholars Publishing.

Dervin, F., & Simpson, A. (2021) *Interculturality and the Political Within Education*. London: Routledge.

Descartes, R. (1968). *Discourse on Method and the Meditations* (Trans. Sutcliffe, F. E.). London: Penguin.

Descartes, R. (2006). *A Discourse on the Method*. Oxford: Oxford University Press.

Duchêne, A., & Heller, M. (Eds.). (2012). *Language in Late Capitalism: Pride and Profit*. New York: Routledge.

Elden, S., Lebas, E., & Kofman, E. (2023). *Henri Lefebvre: Key Writings*. London: Bloomsbury.

Elias, A., & Mansouri, F. (2020). A systematic review of studies on interculturalism and intercultural dialogue. *Journal of Intercultural Studies*, 41(4), 490–523.

Escárcega Zamarrón, S. (2009). Trabajar haciendo: Activist research and interculturalism. *Intercultural Education*, 20(1), 39–50.

Esposito, R. (2008). *Bios: Biopolitics and Philosophy*. Minnesota: University of Minnesota Press.

Espostio, R. (2009). Communitas: The origin and destiny of community (Trans. Timothy Campbell). Stanford: Stanford University Press.

Esposito, R. (2010). *Communitas: The Origin and Destiny of Community*. Stanford: Stanford University Press.

Esposito, R. (2012). *The Third Person: Politics of Life and Philosophy of the Impersonal*. Cambridge: Polity.

Esposito, R. (2015). *Categories of the Impolitical*. New York: Fordham University Press.

Esposito, R. (2017). *The Origin of the Political: Hannah Arendt or Simone Weil*? New York: Fordham University Press.

Esposito, R. (2020). *Vitam instituere*. Retrieved September 20, 2020, from www.journal-psychoanalysis.eu/articles/vitam-instituere/

Fairclough, N. (1992). Discourse and text: Linguistic and intertextual analysis within discourse analysis. *Discourse & Society*, 3(2), 193–217.

Fairclough, N., Jessop, B., & Sayer, A. (2002). Critical realism and semiosis. *Alethia*, 5(1), 2–10.

Federici, S. (2018a). Marx and feminism. *TripleC: Communication, Capitalism & Critique. Open Access Journal for a Global Sustainable Information Society*, 16(2), 468–475.

Federici, S. (2018b). *Re-Enchanting the World: Feminism and the Politics of the Commons*. Oakland, CA: PM Press.

Federici, S. (2020). *Beyond the Periphery of the Skin: Rethinking, Remaking, and Reclaiming the Body in Contemporary Capitalism*. Oakland, CA: PM Press.

Ferri, G. (2018). *Intercultural Communication: Critical Approaches and Future Challenges*. London: Springer.

Ferri, G. (2022). The master's tools will never dismantle the master's house: Decolonising intercultural communication. *Language and Intercultural Communication*, 22(3), 381–390.

Ferri, G. (2023). Embodied others and the ethics of difference. Deterritorialising intercultural learning. *Pedagogy, Culture & Society*, 31(2), 269–282. DOI: 10.1080/14681366.2022.2164340

Flubacher, M. C., & Del Percio, A. (Eds.). (2017). *Language, Education and Neoliberalism: Critical Studies in Sociolinguistics*. Bristol: Multilingual Matters.

Fraser, N., & Jaeggi, R. (2018). *Capitalism: A Conversation in Critical Theory*. London: Verso Books.

Fretheim, K. (2021). Normativity in intercultural communication—What now? *Journal of Multicultural Discourses*, 16(3), 203–209. DOI: 10.1080/17447143.2021.1872584

Gardiner, M. E. (2012). Henri Lefebvre and the 'sociology of boredom'. *Theory, Culture & Society*, 29(2), 37–62.

Giddens, A. (2000). *The Third Way and Its Critics*. Cambridge: Polity.

Gilmore, R. W. (2022). *Abolition Geography: Essays Towards Liberation*. London: Verso Books.

Gray, J., O'Regan, J. P., & Wallace, C. (2018). Education and the discourse of global neoliberalism. *Language and Intercultural Communication*, 18(5), 471–477.

Guilherme, M. (2019). The critical and decolonial quest for intercultural epistemologies and discourses. *Journal of Multicultural Discourses*, 14(1), 1–13. DOI: 10.1080/17447143.2019.1617294

Guilherme, M., & de Souza, L. M. T. M. (Eds.). (2019). *Glocal Languages and Critical Intercultural Awareness: The South Answers Back*. London: Routledge.

Habermas, J. (1987). *The Philosophical Discourse of Modernity: Twelve Lectures*. Cambridge: MIT Press.

Hall, E. T. (1959). *The Silent Language*. New York: Anchor books.

Hall, S. (1985). Signification, representation, ideology: Althusser and the post-structuralist debates. *Critical Studies in Media Communication*, 2(2), 91–114.

Hall, S. (2003). Marx's notes on method: A 'reading' of the '1857 introduction'. *Cultural Studies*, 17(2), 113–149.

Halpern, D. (2005). *Social Capital*. Cambridge: Polity.

Hardt, M. (2009). Politics of the common. Contribution to the Reimagining Society Project hosted by ZCommunications, Boston, 6 July. http://barcelonacomuns.pbworks.com/w/file/fetch/64058130/Hardt_Politics-Common.pdf

Hardt, M. (2010). The common in communism. *Rethinking Marxism*, 22(3), 346–356.

Hardt, M., & Negri, A. (2009). *Commonwealth*. Cambridge: Harvard University Press.

Hardt, M., & Negri, T. (2018). The multiplicities within capitalist rule and the articulation of struggles. *tripleC: Communication, Capitalism & Critique. Open Access Journal for a Global Sustainable Information Society*, 16(2), 440–448.

Hartwig, M. (2011). Bhaskar's critique of the philosophical discourse of modernity. *Journal of Critical Realism*, 10(4), 485–510.

Harvey, D. (1993). From space to place and back again: Reflections on the condition of postmodernity. In Bird, J., Curtis, B., Putnam, T., & Tickner,

L. (Eds.), *Mapping the Futures: Local Cultures, Global Change* (2–29). London: Routledge. https://doi.org/10.4324/9780203977781

Harvey, D. (1996). *Justice, Nature and the Geography of Difference*. London: Blackwell.

Harvey, D. (1998). The body as an accumulation strategy. *Environment and Planning D: Society and Space*, 16(4), 401–421.

Harvey, D. (2000). Cosmopolitanism and the banality of geographical evils. *Public Culture*, 12(2), 529–564.

Harvey, D. (2002). The art of rent: Globalisation, monopoly and the commodification of culture. *Socialist Register*, 38, 93–110.

Harvey, D. (2004). The 'new' imperialism: Accumulation by dispossession. *Socialist Register*, 40, 63–87.

Harvey, D. (2005). The sociological and geographical imaginations. *International Journal of Politics, Culture, and Society*, 18, 211–255.

Harvey, D. (2011). The future of the commons. *Radical History Review*, 2011(109), 101–107.

Harvey, D. (2012). History versus theory: A commentary on Marx's method in Capital. *Historical Materialism*, 20(2), 3–38.

Harvey, D. (2017). *Marx, Capital, and the Madness of Economic Reason*. Oxford: Oxford University Press.

Harvey, D. (2018a). *A Companion to Marx's Capital: The Complete Edition*. London: Verso Books.

Harvey, D. (2018b). *The Limits to Capital*. London: Verso Books.

Harvey, D. (2018c). Universal alienation. *Journal for Cultural Research*, 22(2), 137–150.

Harvey, D. (2018d). Universal alienation and the real subsumption of daily life under capital: A response to Hardt and Negri. *tripleC: Communication, Capitalism & Critique. Open Access Journal for a Global Sustainable Information Society*, 16(2), 449–453.

Harvey, D. (2023). *A Companion to Marx's Grundrisse*. London: Verso Books.

Haug, W. F. (2017). On the need for a new English translation of Marx's Capital. *Socialism and Democracy*, 31(1), 60–86.

Healy, M. (2020). *Marx and Digital Machines*. Westminster: University of Westminster Press.

Heller, M. (2003). Globalization, the new economy, and the commodification of language and identity. *Journal of Sociolinguistics*, 7(4), 473–492.

Heller, M. (2010). The commodification of language. *Annual Review of Anthropology*, 39, 101–114.

Heller, M., & McElhinny, B. (2017). *Language, Capitalism, Colonialism: Toward a Critical History*. Toronto: University of Toronto Press.

Hoff, H. E. (2014). A critical discussion of Byram's model of intercultural communicative competence in the light of bildung theories. *Intercultural Education*, 25(6), 508–517.

Hoff, H. E. (2016). From 'intercultural speaker' to 'intercultural reader': A proposal to reconceptualize intercultural communicative competence through a focus on literary reading. In Dervin, F., & Gross, Z. (Eds.), *Intercultural Competence in Education* (51–71). London: Palgrave Macmillan.

Hofstede, G. (1983). The cultural relativity of organizational practices and theories. *Journal of International Business Studies*, 14(2), 75–89.

Holborow, M. (2018). Language, commodification and labour: The relevance of Marx. *Language Sciences*, 70, 58–67.

Holliday, A. (2011). *Intercultural Communication and Ideology*. London: Sage.

Holliday, A. (2016). Revisiting intercultural competence: Small culture formation on the go through threads of experience. *International Journal of Bias, Identity and Diversities in Education (IJBIDE)*, 1(2), 1–14.

Holliday, A., & Macdonald, M. N. (2020). Researching the intercultural: Intersubjectivity and the problem with postpositivism. *Applied Linguistics*, 41(5), 621–639.

Huang, Z. M. (2021). Intercultural personhood: A non-essentialist conception of individuals for intercultural research. *Language and Intercultural Communication*, 21(1), 83–101.

Issar, S. (2021). Theorising 'racial/colonial primitive accumulation': Settler colonialism, slavery and racial capitalism. *Race & Class*, 63(1), 23–50.

Jack, G. (2004). Language(s), intercultural communication and the machinations of global capital: Towards a dialectical critique. *Language and Intercultural Communication*, 4(3), 121–133.

Jaeggi, R. (2016). What (if anything) is wrong with capitalism? Dysfunctionality, exploitation and alienation: Three approaches to the critique of capitalism. *The Southern Journal of Philosophy*, 54, 44–65.

Kalekin-Fishman, D., & Langman, L. (2015). Alienation: The critique that refuses to disappear. *Current Sociology*, 63(6), 916–933.

Kampmann, D. (2024). Venture capital, the fetish of artificial intelligence, and the contradictions of making intangible assets. *Economy and Society*, 53(1), 39–66. https://doi.org/10.1080/03085147.2023.2294602

Kramsch, C. (2014a). Language and culture. *AILA Review*, 27(1), 30–55.

Kramsch, C. (2014b). Teaching foreign languages in an era of globalization: Introduction. *The Modern Language Journal*, 98(1), 296–311.

Kramsch, C., & Whiteside, A. (2008). Language ecology in multilingual settings. Towards a theory of symbolic competence. *Applied Linguistics*, 29(4), 645–671.

Kramsch, C., & Zhu, H. (2016). Language, culture and language teaching. In Hall, G. (Ed.), *Routledge Handbook of English Language Teaching* (38–50). London: Routledge.

Kramsch, C., & Zhu, H. (2020). Translating culture in global times: An introduction. *Applied Linguistics*, 41(1), 1–9.

Kundnani, A. (2021). The racial constitution of neoliberalism. *Race & Class*, 63(1), 51–69.

Kundnani, A. (2023). *What is Antiracism?: And Why It Means Anticapitalism*. London: Verso Books.

Lacan, J. (1977). *Écrits: A Selection* (Trans. Sheridan, A.). New York: WW Norton.

Ladegaard, H. J., & Phipps, A. (2020). Intercultural research and social activism. *Language and Intercultural Communication*, 20(2), 67–80.

Laplantine, F. (2013). *Quand le moi devient autre: Connaître, partager, transformer*. Paris: CNRS Éditions.

Leeb, C. (2007). Marx and the gendered structure of capitalism. *Philosophy & Social Criticism*, 33(7), 833–859.

Lefebvre, H. (2009). *Dialectical Materialism*. Minneapolis: University of Minnesota Press.

Lefebvre, H. (2014). *Critique of Everyday Life: The One-Volume Edition*. London: Verso Books.

Liddicoat, A. J. (2018). Language teaching and learning as a transdisciplinary endeavour: Multilingualism and epistemological diversity. *AILA Review*, 31(1), 14–28.

Luxemburg, R. (2003). *The Accumulation of Capital* (Trans. Schwarzchild, A., Intro. Kowalik, T.). London: Routledge.

MacDonald, M. N., & O'Regan, J. P. (2013). The ethics of intercultural communication. *Educational Philosophy and Theory*, 45(10), 1005–1017.

Maingueneau, D. (2011). Multiculturality in discourse analysis: The 'French' example. *Journal of multicultural discourses*, 6(2), 105–120.

Mandel, H., & Shalev, M. (2009). Gender, class, and varieties of capitalism. *Social Politics*, 16(2), 161–181.

Martin, J. N., & Nakayama, T. K. (1999). Thinking dialectically about culture and communication. *Communication Theory*, 9(1), 1–25.

Martin, J. N., & Nakayama, T. K. (2013). *Intercultural Communication in Contexts*. New York, NY: McGraw-Hill.

Martin, J. N., & Nakayama, T. K. (2015). Reconsidering intercultural (communication) competence in the workplace: A dialectical approach. *Language and Intercultural Communication*, 15(1), 13–28.

Marx, K. (1972). *The Civil War in France: The Paris Commune*. New York: New World Paperbacks.

Marx, K. (1976). Preface and Introduction to *A Contribution to the Critique of Political Economy*. Beijing: Foreign Languages Press.

Marx, K. (1978). *Capital: A Critique of Political Economy, Volume 2*. London: Penguin.

Marx, K. (1990). *Capital: A Critique of Political Economy, Volume 1*. London: Penguin.

Marx, K. (1991). *Capital: A Critique of Political Economy, Volume 3*. London: Penguin.

Marx, K. (1992). *Early Writings*. London: Penguin.

Marx, K. (1993). *Grundrisse: Foundations of the Critique of political economy*. London: Penguin.

Mata-Benito, P. (2013). Interculturality beyond its own limits: Epistemological and ethical-political proposals. *Anthropology in Action*, 20(3), 43–52.

Matusov, E. (2007). Applying Bakhtin scholarship on discourse in education: A critical review essay. *Educational Theory*, 57(2), 215–237.

McGill, K. (2013). Political economy and language: A review of some recent literature [Review of *Neoliberalism and applied linguistics; Language and late capitalism: Pride and profit; Language as commodity: Global structures, local marketplaces; The sociolinguistics of globalization; The politics of English: A Marxist view of language*, by Block, D., Gray, J., Holborow, M., Duchêne, A., Heller, M., Tan, P. K. W., Rubdy, R., & Blommaert, J.]. *Journal of Linguistic Anthropology*, 23(2), 84–101.

Merleau-Ponty, M. J. J. (1964). *Sense and Non-Sense*. Evanston: Northwestern University Press.

Muth, S., & Del Percio, A. (2018). Policing for commodification: Turning communicative resources into commodities. *Language Policy*, 17, 129–135.

Negri, A. (1996). Twenty theses on Marx: Interpretation of the class situation today. In Makdisi, S., Casarino, C., Karl, R., E. (Eds.), *Marxism Beyond Marxism* (149–180). London: Routledge.

Negri, A. (2017). *Marx and Foucault: Essays*. London: John Wiley & Sons.

Norrie, A. (2010). *Dialectic and Difference: Dialectical Critical Realism and the Grounds of Justice*. London: Routledge.

OECD. (2018). *Preparing Our Youth for an Inclusive and Sustainable World: The OECD PISA Global Competence Framework*. Paris: OECD Library.

O'Kane, C. (2019). Henri Lefebvre and the critical theory of society. In Bauer, J., & Fischer, R., (Eds.), *Perspectives on Henri Lefebvre: Theory, Practices and (Re)Readings* (55–74). Berlin, Boston: De Gruyter Oldenbourg. https://doi.org/10.1515/9783110494983-004

Ollman, B. (1976). *Alienation: Marx's Conception of Man in a Capitalist Society*. Cambridge: Cambridge University Press.

O'Regan, J. P. (2021). *Global English and Political Economy*. London: Routledge.

O'Regan, J. P. (2022). The capitalist dialectics of international student mobility in the modern world-system. *Globalisation, Societies and Education*. DOI: 10.1080/14767724.2022.2095505

Pasquinelli, M. (2023). *The Eye of the Master: A Social History of Artificial Intelligence*. London: Verso Books.

Pêcheux, M. (1982). *Language, Semantics and Ideology: Stating the Obvious* (Trans. Nagpal, H.). London: Palgrave Macmillan.

Pennycook, A. (2021). *Critical Applied Linguistics: A Critical Re-Introduction*. London: Routledge.

Phipps, A. (2013). Intercultural ethics: Questions of methods in language and intercultural communication. *Language and Intercultural Communication*, 13(1), 10–26.

Phipps, A., & Kay, R. (2014). Languages in migratory settings: Place, politics and aesthetics. *Language and Intercultural Communication*, 14(3), 273–286.

Piller, I. (2017). *Intercultural Communication: A Critical Introduction*. Edinburgh: Edinburgh University Press.

Portera, A. (2008). Intercultural education in Europe: Epistemological and semantic aspects. *Intercultural Education*, 19(6), 481–491.

Poulter, S., Riitaoja, A. L., & Kuusisto, A. (2016). Thinking multicultural education 'otherwise'—From a secularist construction towards a plurality of epistemologies and worldviews. *Globalisation, Societies and Education*, 14(1), 68–86.

Ralph, M., & Singhal, M. (2019). Racial capitalism. *Theory and Society*, 48(6), 851–881.

R'boul, H. (2021). North/South imbalances in intercultural communication education. *Language and Intercultural Communication*, 21(2), 144–157.

R'boul, H. (2022a). Epistemological plurality in intercultural communication knowledge. *Journal of Multicultural Discourses*, 17(2), 173–188.

R'boul, H. (2022b). Intercultural philosophy and internationalisation of higher education: Epistemologies of the South, geopolitics of knowledge and epistemological polylogue. *Journal of Further and Higher Education*, 46(8), 1149–1160.

Rehmann, J. (2013). *Theories of Ideology: The Powers of Alienation and Subjection*. Leiden: Brill. https://doi.org/10.1163/9789004252318

Rikap, C. (2021). *Capitalism, Power and Innovation: Intellectual Monopoly Capitalism Uncovered*. London: Routledge.

Roggero, G. (2010). Five theses on the common. *Rethinking Marxism*, 22(3), 357–373.

Roggero, G. (2011). *The Production of Living Knowledge: The Crisis of the University and the Transformation of Labor in Europe and North America*. Philadelphia: Temple University Press.

Ruitenberg, C. W., Knowlton, A., & Li, G. (2016). The productive difficulty of untranslatables in qualitative research. *Language and Intercultural Communication*, 16(4), 610–626.

Said, E. W. (2001). *Reflections on Exile and Other Literary and Cultural Essays*. London: Granta Books.

Scollon, R., Scollon, S. W., & Jones, R. H. (2012). *Intercultural Communication: A Discourse Approach*. London. John Wiley & Sons.

Simpson, A. (2018). Democracy as othering within Finnish education. *International Journal of Bias, Identity and Diversities in Education (IJBIDE)*, 3(2), 77–93.

Simpson, A. (2020). 'I with an[other]', otherness and discourse: Reconstructing 'democracy' through intercultural education. In Dervin, F., Moloney, R., & Simpson, A. (Eds.), *Intercultural Competence in the Work of Teachers: Confronting Ideologies and Practices* (42–56). London: Routledge.

Simpson, A. (2022). Self, reflexivity and the crisis of 'outsideness': A dialogical approach to critical autoethnography in education? In Anteliz, E. A., Mulligan, D. L., & Danaher, P. A. (Eds.), *The Routledge Handbook of Autoethnography in Educational Research* (222–231). London: Routledge.

Simpson, A. (2023). Reconfiguring intercultural communication education through the dialogical relationship of Istina (truth) and Pravda (truth in justice). *Educational Philosophy and Theory*, 55(4), 456–467.

Simpson, A., & Dasli, M. (2023). Concluding remarks on intercultural communication pedagogy and the question of the other. *Pedagogy, Culture & Society*, 31(2), 325–337. DOI: 10.1080/14681366.2022.2164337

Simpson, A., & Dervin, F. (2017). 'Democracy' in education: An omnipresent yet distanced 'other'. *Palgrave Communications*, 3, 24, https://doi.org/10.1057/s41599-017-0012-5

Simpson, A., & Dervin, F. (2019a). Global and intercultural competences for whom? By whom? For what purpose?: An example from the Asia Society and the OECD. *Compare: A Journal of Comparative and International Education*, 49(4), 672–677.

Simpson, A., & Dervin, F. (2019b). The Council of Europe Reference Framework of Competences for Democratic Culture: Ideological refractions, othering and obedient politics. *Intercultural Communication Education*, 2(3), 102–119.

Simpson, A., & Dervin, F. (2020). Forms of dialogism in the Council of Europe Reference Framework on Competences for Democratic Culture. *Journal of Multilingual and Multicultural Development*, 41(4), 305–319.

Simpson, A., Dervin, F., & Tao, J. (2022). Business English students' multifaceted and contradictory perceptions of intercultural communication education (ICE) at a Chinese University. *International Journal of Bilingual Education and Bilingualism*, 25(6), 2041–2057.

Simpson, W., & O'Regan, J. P. (2018). Fetishism and the language commodity: A materialist critique. *Language Sciences*, 70, 155–166.

Singh, S., Bhaskar, R., & Hartwig, M. (2020). *Reality and Its Depths*. Singapore: Springer.

Sorrells, K., & Sekimoto, S. (Eds.). (2015). *Globalizing Intercultural Communication: A Reader*. London: Sage Publications.

Strauss, C. (2006). The imaginary. *Anthropological Theory*, 6(3), 322–344.

Toscano, A. (2008). The open secret of real abstraction. *Rethinking Marxism*, 20(2), 273–287.

Tronti, M. (2009). Towards a critique of political democracy. *Cosmos & History*, 5(1), 68–75.

UNESCO. (2013). *Intercultural Competencies: Conceptual and Operational Framework*. Paris: UNESCO.

Voloshinov, V. N. (1973). *Marxism and the Philosophy of Language* (Trans. Titunik, I. R., & Matejka, L.). Cambridge: Harvard University Press.

Wodak, R. (1999). Critical discourse analysis at the end of the 20th century. *Research on Language & Social Interaction*, 32(1–2), 185–193.

Wodak, R., & Chilton, P. (Eds.). (2005). *A New Agenda in (Critical) Discourse Analysis: Theory, Methodology and Interdisciplinarity*. Amsterdam: John Benjamins Publishing.

World Bank. (2010). *Intercultural Communication*. Washington, DC: World Bank.

World Socialist Web site. (2023). An interview with Harvard anthropology Professor John Comaroff—Part two, May 9, 2023. Retrieved from www.wsws.org/en/articles/2023/05/04/lqga-m04.html

Yohannes, H. T., Phipps, A., Fernandes, F., & Silva, J. (2023). Intercultural knowledge production: Against gender-based violence and towards epistemic justice. *Language and Intercultural Communication*, 23(6), 501–506.

Ypi, L. (2014). On revolution in Kant and Marx. *Political Theory*, 42(3), 262–287.

Ypi, L. (2020). Democratic dictatorship: Political legitimacy in Marxist perspective. *European Journal of Philosophy*, 28(2), 277–291.

Zhang, Y. (2014). *Back to Marx: Changes of Philosophical Discourse in the Context of Economics*. Göttingen: Universitätsverlag Göttingen.

Zhu, H. (Ed.). (2016). *Research Methods in Intercultural Communication: A Practical Guide*. London: John Wiley & Sons.

Zhu, H. (2018). *Exploring Intercultural Communication: Language in Action*. London: Routledge.

Zhu, H. (2020). Making a stance: social action for language and intercultural communication research. *Language and Intercultural Communication*, 20(2), 206–212.

Zotzmann, K. (2017). Research on intercultural communication: A critical realist perspective. In Dasli, M., & Diaz, A. R. (Eds.), *The Critical Turn in Language and Intercultural Communication Pedagogy: Theory, Research and Practice* (99–114). London: Routledge.

Index

abstraction of community 93
abstractions of capital 63
accumulation 54, 59, 82, 99, 103, 104
accumulation by dispossession 109
accumulation of capital 68, 80, 82–6
acritical 4
agency 28, 30, 52, 75
alienation 63–4, 66–70, 87–91
alienation-disalienation 20
alienation-disalienation-new-alienations 72, 91–2, 94–5, 102–4
alien capital 66
alien labour 66, 70
ahistoricises13
annihilation of space through time 58, 82
applied linguistics 23, 31, 46, 75
appropriation 10, 67, 82, 87, 90, 109
Artificial Intelligence 109

belonging 13, 48, 59–62, 67–8
biopolitics 11, 15, 18
bios 18

camera obscura 55
capital 24, 38, 50–4, 58–65, 68–70, 92–3, 103
capitalism 24, 30–1, 35–7, 55–65, 68–70, 80–7, 103
capital-labour relations 68, 70, 98
Cartesian 29, 62
circuits of capital 80–1, 85, 87
circulation of capital 71, 80, 86, 93
class 24, 39, 65, 74, 81–2, 86, 88, 89, 101, 103
classism 111–12
cogito ergo sum 8, 29
commodification of culture 82
commodification of language 56
commodification of social relations 60
commodity 26, 37, 47, 52, 67, 77–8, 86, 90, 98
commodity fetishism 26, 47–8, 52–4, 55–9
commodity-like 20, 36, 59, 71, 77–8
commodity value 80
common 79, 91–7, 102–4
commons as praxis 95, 103, 112
communal life 91, 95
community 6, 14–17, 47, 58, 61–4, 68–72, 78, 93–5, 112
competencies 2, 26, 100
concrete singularity 74
contradictions of capitalism 53, 83
consciousness 7, 28, 88, 90–1
consumption 36–7, 56, 71, 82–3
culturalism 1, 18
culture as a thing 59, 60
culture as commodity-like 78
criticality 4–5, 105
critical discourse analysis 31, 43, 46
critical realism 19–20, 28–9, 37, 40–4, 74–5
critical turn 31, 105

dialectical 38–46, 48–55
dialectical critical realism 42
dialectical materialism 50–51
dialectical method 35, 47
dialectical totality 51, 65, 68, 69, 73–4, 76, 112
dialogism 8, 26
dialogue 13–14
discursive 28, 37, 43–4, 46, 49, 56, 112
division of labour 81, 86–8
dogmatic 9, 23

ecological 50, 51
egocentric 20, 23, 26, 31, 33, 102–3, 112
empiricism 36
epistemic fallacy 29–31, 43, 77, 87–8, 111–12
epistemological break 38
epistemological diversity 90, 101, 104, 105, 112
equality 68, 99, 103
essentialism 2, 38, 55
ethics 24, 43, 99, 104, 105
everyday life 43, 61, 68, 75–6, 79, 80, 86, 89–90, 97, 100, 103
exploitation 65, 82, 109
extra-discursive 43–6

fetishisation 47, 109, 111
fetishised relations 53, 55, 60, 95
fetishism 47, 52–5, 60, 61, 63, 68
Fictitious community 93–4
forms of life 18, 85, 103
freedom 25, 43, 60, 68, 89, 95, 97–9, 104

gender 18, 99, 101, 103
gendered capitalism 86
geographical imagineering 59, 78
geo-historical rhythmics 74
geopolitical 80, 96
global community 17
globalisation 55
global political economy 26, 107

hyper-relativity 105

identification 2, 8, 13, 15, 25
identities 18, 35–36, 59–62
identity 6, 9, 14, 25, 59, 60, 63, 93
ideology 7, 8, 12, 24, 26
imaginary 39, 53, 63, 93
immaterial yet objective 52, 56, 60, 67, 78, 83
immanent contradictions 53
intercultural competence 100, 103
interculturality: definition of 2
interculturality as a transformative commons 99
interdiscursive 10, 13
interpellation 8, 23–5
interpretivist 3, 12, 30
intersectional 18, 99, 101, 107
intersubjectivity 12, 14, 16
intransitive dimension 100–1

Janusian12
judgmental relativism 29

knowing subject 10, 11, 26

labour exploitation 109
labour-power 24, 37, 67, 80–3, 90, 97, 98
language 24, 26, 28, 31, 33, 36, 39–40, 42–6, 54–7, 75–8, 93
language commodification 56
linguism 85, 111, 112
linguistic fallacy 43, 112
logocentrism 22–3

Marxian dialectic 42, 62
Marxism 19, 26, 37, 40, 51, 75, 106
Master-slave 30, 101
materialism 44, 47–51, 61
materialist theory of discourse 23, 31
materiality 20, 36, 37, 42, 43, 45, 94
means of production 73, 80, 84
mental conceptions 48–52, 55, 57, 71, 77
metabolic relation to nature 71, 73
methodological nationalism 3
migration 51, 52, 85

the moments of the materialist dialectic 49
Munchausen Effect: definition of 7; Munchausen Effect and Language 25, 28, 30, 40, 46

new-alienations 88–91, 97, 103
non-essentialist 18, 77
normative 1, 17, 22, 27

ontological irrealism29
ontological monovalence 29–30
ontological struggles 90
ontology 4, 29, 31, 37, 40–4, 74–7, 112
open Marxism 75
open system 73, 75
organic social relations 93
other: definition of 2; self-other relations 2–5
othering 2, 4, 13
otherness 8, 16
overproduction 85

perpetuum mobile 85, 103, 110
Philosophical Discourse of Modernity 26, 28–9, 31, 33, 44, 108
phonocentric 20, 23, 26, 31, 33, 102–3
pluralism 30
political economy: definition of 23–4, 38
political economy and applied linguistics 75–7
political economy and everyday life 79–80, 92–5
political economy and freedom 99–104
political economy and language 23–7
positivism 3, 36, 42
postmodernism 29, 40, 41, 57
postpositvism 3
poststructuralism 23, 29, 75, 105
power relations 4, 10, 25, 30, 43, 44, 46
praxis 46, 87, 91, 95, 99, 101–3
problem of the speaking subject: definition of 23, 31

race 18, 69, 107
racism 19, 85, 86, 87, 91, 111–12
racial capitalism 86, 107
rationalism 11
rationality 11, 12
real: definition of 28, 41–6
real subsumption 96, 98
reflexivity 4, 12, 105
relativity 31, 105
representation: the problem of 6; representation and discourse 14–15, 33, 39–45
reproduction of capital 85–7, 95

selfhood 28
self-liberation 97–8
self-other 2, 4
self-valorise 83
semiotic triangle 43
sign 39
signified 23, 43
signifier 23, 25, 43
spatiotemporal 62
speech 5, 9, 12, 23, 38, 41
social bond 64, 66, 68, 90–2, 102
social inequalities 68, 85, 87, 102, 107, 113
social justice 18, 20, 30, 99–100, 103–5
socially necessary labour 80, 90
social totality 40, 65, 84, 93, 95–7, 110
socio-linguistic 1
solidarity 43, 101
Solidarising Interculturality: definition of 102–4
structure and agency 28, 31, 42
subject of knowledge 39
subjectivity 11, 12, 14–16, 18, 69
Subject-Object 13, 15, 19, 74, 97, 112
Subject-Subject 42, 97, 112
surplus population 85
surplus value 72, 80–4

subsumption: definition of 96–7
subsumption of all forms of life to capital 103
superaddressee 13

transformative praxis 99, 101
transitive dimension 75, 100
technological determinism 50
technological fetishism 109, 111
totality: definition of 50, 65, 85
truth 4, 6, 10, 17, 22–3, 88

unethical 80
unevenness of capitalism 24
unfreedom 68
utterances 4–6, 10, 13

valorisation of capital 68, 83, 84, 109
valorisation of language 23

xenophobia 19, 91, 111

For Product Safety Concerns and Information please contact our EU representative GPSR@taylorandfrancis.com
Taylor & Francis Verlag GmbH, Kaufingerstraße 24, 80331 München, Germany

www.ingramcontent.com/pod-product-compliance
Lightning Source LLC
LaVergne TN
LVHW010926110826
845149LV00013B/2501
* 9 7 8 1 0 3 2 2 5 5 2 4 8 *